IN SEARCH OF
CERTAINTY

INSEARCHOF

TYNDALE HOUSE PUBLISHERS, INC.

Wheaton, Illinois

CERTAINTY

JOSH MCDOWELL
& THOMAS WILLIAMS

Visit Tyndale's exciting Web site at www.tyndale.com

In Search of Certainty

Cover designed by Kirk DouPonce, UDG Designworks.

Interior designed by Zandrah Maguigad

Edited by Lynn Vanderzalm

Library of Congress Cataloging-in-Publication Data

McDowell, Josh.
   In search of certainty / Josh McDowell, Thomas Williams.
     p. cm.
Includes bibliographical references.
   ISBN 0-8423-7972-X (pbk.)
   1. God—Proof, Cosmological.   2. Truth—Religious aspects—Christianity.   I. Williams, Thomas.
II. Title.
   BT103.M33 2003
231'.042—dc21   2003006861

Printed in the United States of America

08   07   06   05   04   03
8   7   6   5   4   3   2   1

TO TERRY BOUCHELLE AND LYNDON LATHAM

CONTENTS

Acknowledgments. ix

CHAPTER ONE: **DOES IT MATTER WHAT I BELIEVE?** 1
THE TRUTH ABOUT TRUTH
Mere belief does not provide certainty. Certainty comes from
assurance that what we believe is objectively true.

CHAPTER TWO: **WHERE SHALL I BASE MY BELIEF?** 15
THE NEED FOR AN ULTIMATE ABSOLUTE
Certainty must be based on the bedrock of the ultimate absolute
for truth: God himself.

CHAPTER THREE: **CAN I TRUST WHAT I THINK?** 29
THE ABSOLUTE FOR REASON
Human reason, based on the absolute of a rational God, is a valid
instrument in the search for certainty.

CHAPTER FOUR: **WHO DECIDES WHAT IS RIGHT?** 45
THE ABSOLUTE FOR MORALITY
The universal sense of morality provides certainty of the existence
of God, whose character defines goodness.

CHAPTER FIVE: **WHAT'S THE POINT OF IT ALL?** 63
THE ABSOLUTE FOR MEANING
The inherent sense of meaning in the universe provides certainty
that a transcendent God exists.

CHAPTER SIX: **WHY DO WE LOVE SUNSETS AND SYMPHONIES?** 75
THE ABSOLUTE FOR BEAUTY
The pervading awareness of beauty and joy in the universe
encourages certainty that a transcendent, loving God exists.

CHAPTER SEVEN: **IS THE UNIVERSE A COSMIC ACCIDENT?** 95
THE IRRATIONALITY OF EVOLUTION
The unscientific irrationality of evolution undermines certainty,
leaving us with unanswerable questions about origins and destiny.

CHAPTER EIGHT: **THE RATIONAL LEAP OF FAITH** 117
THE RELATIONSHIP BETWEEN FAITH AND REASON
A rational, confident step of faith in God leads us to know with
certainty that he exists.

CHAPTER NINE: **HOW CAN I KNOW GOD?** 131
FINDING CERTAINTY IN RELATIONSHIP
Faith based on reason leads us to experience the certainty of God
in a loving relationship with him.

Notes. 147
Revolutionary Beyond Belief Resources 150
About the Authors 155

ACKNOWLEDGMENTS

Few books get off the ground without the lift provided by the talents of numerous people. This book is no exception. We willingly express our gratitude to several whose contributions have greatly enhanced the value and effectiveness of these pages:

Dave Bellis, our longtime friend and associate who established our initial contact, cleared the path, and guided the collaborative process, working with both authors and the publisher in managing the business details, the workflow, and the creative growth of the project.

Lynn Vanderzalm of Tyndale House, for her editorial partnership and willingness to struggle with the authors over individual sentences and words to assure just the right meaning. Ed Stewart, whose suggestions did much to increase the readability of some of the abstract concepts presented in this book. Ron Beers, Ken Petersen, and Jon Farrar of Tyndale House for their oversight and management of the process.

Dr. William Lane Craig, Keith Cox, and Dr. Ravi Zacharias for their review, insightful analysis, and critique of the philosophic and theological concepts presented in this book.

Gene Shelburne, Pat Flynn, Tommy Williams, Sam Means, and Jay Latham—a mix of ministers, laymen, teachers, scientists, and even an agnostic who read the manuscript at various stages and offered valuable suggestions for improvement.

Kirk DouPonce of UDG Designworks for the excellent cover design.

And finally, the many Tyndale House people for handling all the unsung but vital details required to bring a book into the market—copyediting, internal design and layout, production, marketing, and promotion.

We thank all of you very much.

JOSH McDOWELL
THOMAS WILLIAMS

CHAPTER ONE

DOES IT MATTER WHAT I BELIEVE?

THE TRUTH ABOUT TRUTH

One evening at a denominational youth conference, I was
speaking to a crowd of high school and college-age young
people.* These were not ordinary Christian kids; they were the
brightest and most exceptional from their churches, handpicked by
their leaders. I wanted to find out just how firm and knowledgeable
these students were in their Christian beliefs. So at one point in the
conference, I took a cordless microphone and waded into the crowd
of lively, radiant faces.

Approaching one young man, I held up my Bible and asked,
"Do you believe the Bible is the Word of God?"

"Yes!" he said with confidence and conviction.

I probed him further. "Do you believe the Bible is true?"

"Yes!" rang the answer again.

*The personal experiences related in this book come from the lives of both Josh McDowell and Tom Williams. Since inserting parenthetical references to differentiate the authors can be both cumbersome and distracting, we opted not to do it.

Then I asked, "Is it historically accurate and reliable?"

"Of course!" he replied with confidence.

Then I lowered my voice and asked him, "Why?"

He looked back at me, shrugged his shoulders, and said, "That's a tough one."

I turned to another student and fired the same questions. He also enthusiastically agreed that the Bible is the true Word of God. But when I asked why he believed it, he also drew a blank.

It was the same with every student I interviewed that night. Each confidently affirmed belief in the Bible, but not one of them could tell me *why* he or she believed. Though these young people were the cream of the crop in their denomination, when it came to understanding the basis for their belief, they were stumped.

The next day at the morning session, a young man—I'll call him Darren—came up to me, bursting with excitement. "I know the answer," he said.

He caught me off guard, and I wasn't sure what he meant. "The answer to what?" I asked.

"The answer to your question about why the Bible is true."

"Wonderful," I said. "Let's hear it."

"Because I believe it," Darren replied.

I wanted to be sure I understood his point. I said, "Come again?"

He held up his Bible and said, "It is true because I believe it." He beamed as if he had just won a new Ferrari. The young people who had gathered around him smiled and nodded in enthusiastic agreement. A great mystery had apparently been solved.

I asked him, "Does this mean that the Bible would also be true for other kids in your school?"

"It is if they believe it," Darren responded.

I gazed at him for a moment. "Do you know the basic difference between you and me?" I asked. "To you the Bible is true because you believe it. For me, I believe the Bible because it is true."

WHICH COMES FIRST: TRUTH OR BELIEF?

At first glance, my statement to this young Christian may sound as petty and insignificant as the debate over which came first, the chicken or the egg. Both eggs and chicken are regular items on the menu in most homes, and as long as they nourish us, why bother with which came first? Similarly, both belief and truth work together as vital elements in an ongoing relationship with God. Does it matter which comes first? Is one really more important than the other?

Yes, the difference I pointed out to Darren between these two approaches to belief and truth is significant. In fact, these views are diametrically opposed; you can't have it both ways. I assert that the Bible is inherently true even if one chooses not to believe it. Darren thinks the Bible is true for him or his friends *because* they believe it. I contend that truth is already established and we must respond to it with faith. His position is that we create truth by what we choose to believe. I say that truth is absolute. In Darren's mind, truth is arbitrary. I say that truth exists as an objective reality outside ourselves and that it is true for all people, at all times, and in all places. Darren says that truth is fluid and adaptable to one's own internal belief system. The difference between these two views is not merely an abstract theological point; it has far-reaching practical implications. Make no mistake: What you believe about the nature of truth will determine whether or not you find and experience certainty in your life.

Young people like Darren may feel some sense of certainty about their unexamined beliefs in the morning of their lives simply because life is full of hope and promise. Caught up in the busyness and energy of youth, few find the time to check out what they believe and why. But this unexamined sense of certainty will not carry them far. Sooner or later everyone's beliefs will be tested by jarring encounters with reality. At that point certainty will evaporate unless it is grounded firmly in absolute truth.

In today's world, people are becoming less concerned with truth than with certainty. They see truth as an abstract concept that is perhaps of little practical concern. But they crave a sense of certainty because it gives them a feeling of security. That feeling may be unwarranted because people can feel certainty about beliefs that are false. And they can lack certainty about beliefs that are true. Actually, it's not really certainty that we should be searching for but a way to know solid truth. Knowing truth and knowing why you believe it will give you lasting certainty. You may feel certainty for a while without examining your beliefs, but at the end of the day no real, lasting certainty is possible unless you know your beliefs are firmly grounded in absolute truth. So, the search for certainty is really a search for truth. When people understand the absoluteness of truth—when they have solid reason to know that what they believe is truth—certainty will follow.

Darren's view of truth and belief is not an obscure blip on the radar screen of current thinking among Christian youth. A Newsweek cover story titled "What Teens Believe" tells of Rob Rienow, a youth minister at Wheaton Bible Church, Wheaton, Illinois, asking a gathering of Christian young people, "Who do you think God is? What is he like?"

Their answers were as individual as the kids themselves.
One thought God was like his grandfather: "He's there, but

I never see him." Another took a harder view, describing "an evil being who wants to punish me all the time." Two more opinions followed. Finally, the last teen weighed in: "I think you're all right, because that's what you really believe." In other words, as Rienow relates it, God is whatever works for you. On this, all of the youth agreed.[1]

It's not only young people who are losing a solid sense of absolute truth today. While speaking in another conference, I approached a youth pastor in the audience. He had been pointed out to me as one of the most outstanding, astute, and best theologically trained of all that denomination's youth workers. I asked him the same question I had asked Darren, and his answer was the same as Darren's: "Because I have faith." It appears that those who lead and train our young people have adopted the idea that the mere exercise of faith creates a working truth for each individual.

This pattern of thought now pervades not only the younger generations but also American society as a whole. It's no wonder our kids grow up assuming they must determine what is right for themselves. The world has convinced them that truth does not exist apart from what they decide truth is.

It was not always this way, of course. Up until about two centuries ago, most people generally accepted that simple faith in God and implicit trust in the Bible were the primary avenues to truth. Then came the Age of Enlightenment in the eighteenth century, when human reason supplanted faith as the surer road to truth. The existence of God and the authority of the Bible began to be questioned more openly. Modernism grew out of the Enlightenment, claiming scientific deduction to be the only dependable method for determining objective truth. Those influenced by the modernist tendency insisted that science alone could determine what can be known. The existence of God was further placed in doubt because it could not be proven by scientific methods. Creation as the explanation for the existence of every living thing on the earth was replaced by the more palatable theory of evolution.

THE POSTMODERN AGE: CREATE YOUR OWN TRUTH

In the last two or three decades, postmodernism has edged out modernism as the prevailing mode of thought influencing our culture, casting a dark shadow over both reason and the scientific method. Postmodernism is a worldview that asserts that external, absolute truth—that is, a truth that is true for all people, in all places, and at all times—cannot be known through reason or science because truth is either nonexistent or unknowable. Postmodern thought asserts that experience is more reliable than reason. Reason, claims the postmodernist, is fogged and contaminated by worldviews, prejudices, environment, and upbringing, all of which render it undependable as an instrument for grasping absolute truth. Therefore, says the postmodernist, the idea of truth is *created* rather than *discovered*. Postmodernists' personal experiences define their needs and shape their answers to those needs. In spite of their belief that we can't really know truth, they understand that all individuals must have some sort of working philosophy as a framework for their thought and values. Therefore they must create their own truths based on what works for them. In a nutshell, postmodernists say, "If it's true for you, then it's as true as it needs to be. And no one has the right to question what you have chosen as truth for yourself."

So we can see where people like Darren are coming from. Darren's generation has lived its entire existence within the postmodern age, and their thinking shows it. Postmodernism now shapes the attitudes of our society as a whole, even though most people don't even know the meaning of the word. Like Darren, today's kids are deeply influenced by the subtle but persistent and growing view that every individual is free to determine for himself or herself what is right and what is true.

And it's not only the younger generations that are affected. Don't be surprised to meet many adults or even Christians who are reluctant to draw a line between right and wrong or to affirm a belief in absolute truth. It seems that few people today give much thought to why they think as they do; they simply think as they are led by our culture. They have adopted a postmodern mind-set by default, latching onto a convenient and acceptable worldview that seems to work for them without bothering to check whether it is based in truth—or even needs to be. They may be unaware that truth matters enough to make any real difference in the way they live. Perhaps if they were pressed for an explanation of why they believe as they do, they might offer one that borders on New Age mysticism: "If you believe anything strongly enough, the universe [or God] will endorse it." They feel there is some inherent power in the nature of a strongly held belief that moves the powers that be to bring reality into alignment with it, just as parents affirm their children's faith in Santa Claus by being sure they find presents under the tree on Christmas morning.

Let us state as clearly as possible the premise that we will develop throughout this book: Absolute truth is an objective reality that exists totally independent of what anyone thinks or feels about it. It is a reality that is true for all people, for all times, for all places. Truth is real and solid whether or not we choose to believe it, just as Mount Everest is real and solid whether or not we choose to climb it. Contrary to postmodern thought, we do not *create* truth; we *discover* it. Belief does not determine reality; reality exists apart from belief. Our belief in the truth merely brings us into alignment with it and activates its power in our lives.

WHAT IS TRUE VS. WHAT IS TRUE FOR YOU

If mere belief determined reality, it would matter little what anyone believes. For the person who chooses to believe in Christ and the Bible, Christianity would become the truth. But for the person who chooses to believe in the Koran and Muhammad, Islam would become the truth. The same could be said about any other religion, sect, or cult. If belief determined reality, whatever god a person chose to believe in would become god for that person. And for the atheist, reality would consist of a universe with no god at all. In the postmodern world, all these "truths" are considered equal because truth is whatever a person chooses to believe. As long as it's "true for you," then it's true.

But we must ask, does the phrase "true for you" really mean anything? Can truth exist as a reality solely for the persons who believe it and for no one else? Consider a simple illustration. You and your friend find an apple on the table. Your friend believes it is full of worms, but you believe it is fresh and worm-free. Can your differing beliefs about the apple create two different truths that each of you can experience as reality? The way to find out is to slice the apple open. Then you will discover that either the apple has worms or it doesn't. The moment you slice into it, either your "truth" or that of your friend will be exposed as error. The truth about the apple is independent of whatever either of you may believe about it.

No one employs mere belief when dealing with the down-to-earth realities of everyday life. For example, none of us would buy a used car assuming the truth of the salesperson's enthusiastic pitch that it's in excellent running condition. We would have it checked out by a reputable mechanic or insist on a generous warranty. We all know that *believing* a car to be in tiptop shape doesn't make it so. Or if a stranger offered you an unknown pill, guaranteeing that it would cure your migraine headaches, you wouldn't swallow it on the spot. We don't take pills unless they are prescribed by a trusted physician and prepared by a licensed pharmacist. It doesn't matter how much we *believe* they will work or want them to work; we know that the wrong pills won't help us and could even harm us.

In making everyday life decisions, we insist that truth precede belief. We don't trust our lives and health to what we hope, dream, wish, or think will happen. Our beliefs are conditioned on dependable, objective, verifiable truth. "True for you" doesn't work for any of us in the material world. We insist on going beyond belief to what is objectively true.

THE TRUTH ABOUT RELIGIOUS EXPERIENCE

Why do we abandon rational objectivity when it comes to matters of religion? Why do people in general and believers like Darren in particular focus their attention on the *act* of belief while minimizing *what* they should believe? It is likely that they do not see religion as part of their real world. They consider religion to be vague, abstract, ethereal, and unknowable. They don't classify it as a hard reality in the same category as buying a car or swallowing a pill. In their minds they have drawn a line separating practical realities from these distant abstractions, and they feel no need to apply the same rigid standard to determine their truth. This is their mistake. These abstract realities that seem so distant and unknowable are actually more important and have more impact on you than whether you eat a wormy apple. Infinitely more is at stake in believing the wrong "truth" about God than in swallowing the wrong prescription medication. If there is a personal, absolute God who exists as a reality independent of our belief, his claims must be seriously investigated by a standard at least as hard-nosed as we would apply when buying a car. A right relationship with him is crucial to our ultimate destiny.

It is likely that most unbelievers who turn to religion are not at first interested in truth or their ultimate destiny. Their concern is more immediate and practical. They are desperate for answers to their problems, strength for their weakness, and stability in their relationships. They are searching for certainty in a painful and uncertain world. So they choose a belief system that seems to meet their most pressing needs, regardless of that system's truth claims. For example:

- Maria is having trouble with her two teenagers. Members of a pseudo-Christian cult come to her door touting their church's strong emphasis on family values and youth activities. To Maria, who has her hands full working a job and bringing up two teenagers alone, all churches are basically the same. So she joins the one that promises to help her rescue her kids. It doesn't matter to Maria that this cult's doctrine has no regard for ultimate truth.
- Randall, a top-level executive, has a high-stress job that is spiking his blood pressure. His doctor urges him to try yoga and meditation to control the stress and anxiety in his life. Randall meets another executive who seems to have it all together. This man swears by the meditation techniques taught by an Eastern guru. Randall joins the guru's group, which is steeped in the Hindu religion.

People like Maria and Randall will stick with a belief system as long at it works for them. They will blindly accept whatever promises to ease their burdens, solve their problems, and provide an element of certainty in their lives with little or no regard for whether there is any ultimate reality behind the promise. But when they don't find the peace and relief they seek, they will jump the fence to the greener pasture that seems to offer a "truth" that works better for them.

Ultimately, those who hold to a personal belief that is not grounded in absolute truth will come away empty. No mere belief, no matter how sincerely held, can provide long-term certainty, meet human needs, and solve physical, emotional, or relational problems. Just as a phone call is futile unless there is someone on the other end of the line, a belief is futile unless there is a reality out there to validate it. When our belief reaches out, there must be a hand reaching back. To do us any good, reality must be more than a phantom projected by wishful thinking masquerading as faith; it must exist objectively. The only kind of God that can meet our needs is a God who is real—a God with whom we can make a solid connection and establish a relationship.

People can affirm various "truths" only if they really believe in none of them. Only if you believe that no real truth is available can you affirm the efforts of everyone to construct his or her own truth. To say that one truth is as good as another is to say that it really doesn't matter what you believe because all religious beliefs are mere coping illusions that we grasp in desperation to help us get through the uncertainties and mystifications of life. People cannot affirm all truths if they have any notion that one real truth actually exists.

But what happens to the idea that we can create our own truth if that one real God actually does exist? What if there is a God out there, a God who is the only source of certainty, meaning, purpose, and identity? And what if, as Christianity affirms, there is only one road by which you can reach him and that is through a relationship with the person of Jesus Christ? We are fully aware that the claims of Christianity are exclusive and make no allowance for other gods or other ways to God. But in spite of the fact that people find Christianity unattractive because it seems to be intolerant of other views and in spite of the fact that its exclusive claims are currently considered to be politically incorrect, what if they just happen to be true? What would that do to the notion that we should affirm all beliefs as valid?

It would kill it.

If there is one, solid absolute truth, then the idea that we can create our own truth is fatal. It is the most dangerous doctrine we can adopt because if you hold to a belief that does not exist as an objective reality, you are in jeopardy of missing out on the promises and benefits of knowing the real God. You are in danger of throwing away your life.

If you believe that a real truth may exist out there somewhere but it is impossible for you to know it, the answer is not to throw up your hands and adopt some convenient imitation of truth that seems to work for you; you must keep searching. If real truth exists, no substitute will give you the answers you need.

THE SEARCH FOR CERTAINTY

Here at the outset of this book, we make no secret about our conviction that Christianity presents the only accurate picture of reality. Our purpose is to counter the postmodern view and show that this truth is certain and founded on solid absolutes. And the ultimate absolute that gives us certainty is nothing less than a personal God who invites us into a relationship with him. Truth is not an abstract concept that can change as our needs change. Truth resides within the person of God, whose existence and character is solid, unchangeable, and absolute. Truth is not arbitrary; it flows from God's nature. All alternative religions and all attempts to create one's own truth are illusions that have no reality and thus lead inevitably to dead ends.

We will show that absolutes are real, that truth is valid, and that faith in God is not an irrational leap into the dark or a desperate hope without substance. Rather, such faith is utterly rational, soundly grounded, intellectually defensible, and emotionally fulfilling. You don't have to check your brains at the door of the church to become a believer. And you don't have to turn your back on life's joys. To the contrary, the God of creation is the only complete, rational answer to people's religious and philosophic questions, and a personal relationship with him is the only source of real happiness.

Even as we take you to the bedrock of truth and demonstrate the rationality of faith in God, we fully understand that few people are won to belief by sheer reason. It seems that most come to him through the testimony of someone who cares about them and whose life radiates such joy and confidence that the unbeliever's mouth waters to have the same thing. We must never let this avenue to faith be a target for our disdain. Some of the strongest, finest, surest, and most dedicated Christians we know became believers because of someone's testimony before they discovered the rational underpinnings of their faith. Many other people, however, wouldn't think of believing in God until they feel the solid foundation of truth under their feet.

Whichever you are—a person drawn to God through the life or testimony of a friend or one kicking the tires and looking under the hood of the Christian faith, we hope that this book will help you see that the foundations of Christianity are firm and solid.

1. Why is it vital that truth precede belief?
2. What are the central tenets of truth taught by the Enlightenment, modernism, and postmodernism?
3. Can belief alone determine truth? Why or why not?
4. Can truth be true for one person but not for another? Why or why not?
5. What can happen when people focus on *the act of* belief instead of *what they believe*?
6. Can the existence of God be proven? Why or why not?
7. Can a strongly held belief without content meet actual needs? Explain.

CHAPTER TWO

WHERE SHALL I BASE MY BELIEF?

I don't believe in absolutes of any kind, moral or otherwise," said Kevin as he and his long-time friend Corey drove down the road along a California beach. Both were students at UCLA, with graduation less than a year away. Corey had just suggested that Kevin's one-night stand with the unknown girl he had picked up at a party last night was wrong because it violated the standards of morality.

"Those standards may have been necessary for the stability of societies in the unenlightened past, but they are out of date today," Kevin insisted. "We don't need such standards anymore." All standards are arbitrary, and none are absolute. We should do away with them.

At the next exit Kevin drove off the freeway, turned into a shopping center, and parked his convertible in front of the Surf Shop. "Here we are," he said as the two young men got out of the car and entered the store. Kevin was looking for a new surfboard. He and Corey looked at several before he found one he liked.

"How long is the blue one there?" he asked the salesperson.

"It's eight feet, six inches," replied the clerk.

Kevin looked hard at the board. "I think you must be mistaken. It sure doesn't look that long," he said.

The clerk insisted that the length he had quoted was accurate and even showed Kevin the tag to confirm it. But Kevin was sure there was a mistake. "Do you have a tape measure?" he asked.

The clerk brought out a steel tape and helped Kevin measure the surfboard as Corey held it horizontally for them. "I guess you are right," admitted Kevin, scratching his head. "It just doesn't look that long to me." He took out his wallet and handed his credit card to the clerk. "I'll take it," he said.

After the two young men loaded the surfboard and got into Kevin's car, Corey grinned at his friend and said, "I thought you didn't believe in any kind of absolute standards."

"I don't," insisted Kevin.

"Then why did you ask for a tape measure to check the size of the surfboard?"

"I didn't want to get cheated. I wanted to be sure of the length."

"And you needed a standard to be sure. The tape is a standard for linear measurement. So you see, you do believe in standards."

"Oh, come on, Corey. That's different, and you know it."

"Is it really? You just showed that we would live in a world of chaos and uncertainty if we didn't have standards for linear measurement. Isn't it possible that there are also standards for behavior? For the way we should treat people?"

Corey is right. A world without standards would be a world of chaos. According to tradition, no standards for linear measurements existed a few centuries ago. Every carpenter sized his lumber by the handiest measuring device available—his own foot. As a result, six-foot wooden tables came in various lengths because carpenter's feet came in various lengths. Customers who wanted the most value for their money probably took care to check their carpenter's shoe size before signing a contract.

As the legend has it, the king decided to end the uncertainty about linear measurements. He marked and published the size of his own royal foot and decreed that all carpenters must henceforth use its length as the standard for a one-foot rule. From then on, all people ordering a six-foot table in his land knew exactly what they were getting: a table exactly six times the length of the king's foot.

Just as the legendary king provided a standard for linear measurements in his kingdom, governments today provide standards for such things as the weights and measures we use in everyday interactions and commerce. In the United States, these standards are set by an agency called the U.S. Bureau of Standards. This agency maintains fixed standards for the specific volume of gallons, quarts, and pints; the specific weight of tons, pounds, and ounces; the specific length of miles, yards, and inches.

Though we think little about these standards or their sources, we depend on them every day in practical ways. They assure us that when we purchase a pound of nails, two yards of fabric, or a quart of milk, we know exactly how much product we will take home. Or when we travel from Dallas to Nashville at a given rate of speed, we can determine how long the trip will take.

CONDITIONAL STANDARDS AND ABSOLUTES

These standards that governments set serve us well, but they are not absolute; they are what we will call for our present purposes *conditional* standards. They are conditional on the authority that sets them. These standards can change when the authority behind them changes. A new king may come to power and decide that his size-fourteen foot makes a better standard than his predecessor's size ten. European governments have changed the standards for all weights and lengths to the metric system and the medium of exchange from the currency of individual countries to the common Euro. Yet in spite of such changes, we accept these conditional standards and the authority behind them because we know we need commonly accepted standards to facilitate commerce.

When we look beneath some of our conditional standards, we find deeper unconditional standards rooted in realities more reliable than human authority. The standards we use to measure time, for example, are not conditional because they are beyond human control. Nature, rather than human edict, dictates the lengths of days and years. A day will always be one cycle of daylight and darkness, and a year will always consist of 365 days. Somewhere back in history some authority decided to divide the day into twenty-four segments called hours, but these segments had to conform to a larger reality over which humans had no authority—the rotation of the earth. Hours and minutes are conditional standards, but they had to conform to an unconditional standard that is not subject to human decision or manipulation. Tracing such standards back to their authoritative or foundational sources gives them a solid reason to be trusted as dependable.

Not only do we need authoritative sources for the standards that keep society functioning or for the measurement of time, we also need them to validate most of our knowledge and beliefs. The conditional standards of government work just fine for such practical things as weights, measures, and mediums of exchange. The unconditional standards that nature provides are perfectly adequate to give us a reliable way to measure time. But we have questions, and we have a need for knowledge that reaches far deeper than what either government or nature can validate.

We humans are saddled with persistent questions about our own meaning, destiny, and purpose. We want assurance that such abstract values as love, truth, beauty, fair play, and goodness are real. We want assurance of the reality of the things we perceive with our senses—trees, mountains, birds, and people. We want assurance that the conclusions we reason out and think through with our minds are valid. To assure us that such beliefs are true, we need a standard more solid than any king's decree and more reliable than the orbits of planets. We need a standard that is unconditional. We need an absolute.

Webster's Collegiate Dictionary defines *absolute* as "perfect, unquestionable, fundamental, ultimate."[1] An absolute is rock-bottom truth or a ground of knowledge that is beyond question. It is the final authority. It is what we use as proof when anything is challenged. An absolute backs up what we know and gives confidence and a reason for certainty to our knowledge. An absolute must stand beyond challenge to function as a reliable standard. It must be fixed, constant, and taken for granted.

To be certain that any belief is true, we must find beneath it an ultimate absolute that it rests on. We must know there exists a final authority beyond question to serve as the ultimate answer to all questions. We must know there exists a foundational truth that explains all truth. Our claim to knowledge collapses like a line of falling dominoes unless it ultimately runs up against something that can't be knocked over. Before we can determine whether our beliefs are objectively true, we must determine that they are backed up by something so obviously true that it needs no proof of its own.[2]

Many of the beliefs we listed above seem so obviously true that we are surprised that anyone would question them. Love, truth, beauty, reason, fair play, and objective reality seem to exist as self-evident truths without needing absolutes to support them. But today it seems that no truth is self-evident enough to be safely beyond question. Love, in the minds of many, does not really exist. It is merely an instinct or a hormonal reaction that nature has given us to preserve the race. Many believe that beauty has no objective existence but is a subjective interpretation in the eye of the beholder. Society increasingly doubts whether truth is absolute. The postmodern mind-set has conditioned many to see it as conditional and changeable, depending on the time, place, and circumstance. If truth is not supported by an absolute, one belief is as good as another, and none can be held up as truly right to the exclusion of all others.

Without an absolute, even the apparent fact that we exist is not a certainty. One doctrine of some Eastern religions says that existence is an illusion. What seems real to us—including our own being—is merely a dream in the mind of a great, impersonal, cosmic consciousness. And to people who operate within this assumption, it is very difficult to give proof to the contrary. Everything that would prove to them that reality is objective is merely a part of the dream. Pinching themselves to wake up would prove nothing. They would insist that they merely dreamt they woke up.

We may dismiss such a view of reality as unfounded and irrational, but how can we know for sure? How can we prove whether what we call reality is fact or illusion? whether beauty is real or subjective? whether reason can give us accurate conclusions about truth? How can we be sure there is even such a thing as truth? Facing such choices is like facing a hallway lined with unmarked doors, all alike, all unlocked, any of which may lead us either to solid, dependable truth or into a void of irrationality and delusion. How do we choose which door to enter?

One little first-grade girl had an answer. A classmate brought a two-week-old puppy to school for show and tell. In the discussion that followed, the children began to wonder about the gender of the dog, but they were uncertain about how to determine it. The little girl raised her hand, "I know how we can tell," she said. The teacher, resigning herself to a discussion of the birds and the bees, replied, "How can we tell, Megan?" The girl answered, "We can vote."

We may chuckle at the story, but it illustrates an operating assumption held by much of the population of the United States. The democratic ideal of majority rule, augmented by the principles of equality and tolerance, has led many to accept the principle that whatever society endorses carries the weight of truth. Controversial practices such as abortion, homosexuality, euthanasia, and sexual freedom become right if society as a whole says they are right. Many people today insist that they have as much right to adopt these values as those of fidelity, chastity, love, and fair play. They see no real difference in the validity of either list, and they have no way to determine it except by mutual consent of the majority. To them, absolutes are unimportant or nonexistent. They conclude that we decide for ourselves what we want to believe on the basis of our own convenience.

If there is an ultimate absolute that determines the shape of our lives in the same way that the rotation of the earth determines the length of a day, it is perilous to ignore it. To do so would put us out of alignment with the way the universe is set up. If an ultimate absolute exists, we will find it impossible to build a stable life on any other foundation, even though society as a whole may consider other foundations to be perfectly adequate. Government, with its finger to the wind of the majority, has no more right—and ultimately no more ability—to legislate changes to the universal basics of morality than to legislate changes to the length of a day. Reality will not budge one inch to satisfy the whims of a self-serving society. Any apparent success in changing moral principles or core truth is a temporary illusion that will soon shatter into grief and chaos. As we will show, real truth is solid and immovable. It is rigidly supported by an absolute that is not conditional or subject to change of any kind.

FINDING THE ULTIMATE ABSOLUTE

The only safe way to determine whether our beliefs are true is to assure ourselves that they rest on a solid, dependable foundation. We must look beneath each belief, layer by layer, until we find the absolute that supports it. We place confidence in our beliefs in much the same way that we place confidence in our houses. We trust the second story because it is built on a strong and dependable first story. We trust the first story because it is built on a strong and dependable foundation. We trust the foundation because it is built on strong and dependable bedrock. We trust bedrock because—well, everyone trusts bedrock. It is futile to question bedrock or look beneath it for something more solid. Experience, reason, and intuition all tell us that bedrock is the builder's ultimate answer to solidity. We've seen houses built on bedrock all our lives, and they are still standing. It would be silly to spend time and money to analyze bedrock by digging through it to prove what everyone already knows: bedrock is solid, dependable, and safe to build on. Bedrock is the builder's absolute.

The process is the same when it comes to validating our deepest beliefs and convictions. Reason tells us to look beneath our beliefs layer by layer until at the bottom of the stack we find a foundational truth we feel we can safely assume to be true—a truth beyond empirical proof, a truth that we accept as logically necessary or too obvious to question.

The process of working our way through these layers goes something like this: We believe it is right to help stranded motorists because we accept the validity of the maxim "do to others what you would have them to do to you." We believe this maxim to be valid because it is rooted in our understanding that we are mutually dependent on each other for survival in a world filled with trouble and pain. We believe that we should take this mutual dependence seriously as necessary to survival because we accept without question the universal belief that society should be preserved. Virtually everyone accepts this truth as foundational. It is a universally assumed absolute adopted by all societies in all places and in all times.

Yet even this absolute stops one step short of being bedrock. Why should society be preserved? Who came up with that idea? Why does it matter? Why do we think we should believe it? Before we can trust even this seemingly obvious foundational truth to be really true, we must look beneath it to see if it has the bedrock support of an ultimate absolute. And if we find such an absolute, we can lay proofs aside and dig no deeper. We have reached the bedrock truth that must simply be accepted as a logical necessity too obvious to question.

TRUSTING THE ULTIMATE ABSOLUTE

A thoroughgoing rationalist may be disturbed by the suggestion that an ultimate absolute stands beyond the reach of proof. If we are rational creatures looking for a rational method to validate our deepest beliefs, shouldn't we be wary of the suggestion to lay reason aside and merely accept this ultimate absolute without proof? How can we know the bedrock beneath our beliefs is really solid if reason can't prove it?

We don't suggest that in making this assumption, we should lay reason aside. Indeed, reason itself shows us that there is no alternative to making it. The ultimate absolute cannot be proved because if it could be proved, it would not be the ultimate absolute. It would be only a conditional standard in need of validation by a deeper, self-evident truth, which would actually be the ultimate absolute. That which cannot be proven can only be accepted or rejected. But it should not be accepted blindly. Before we place our trust in the ultimate absolute, reason should show us that it is a logical necessity with no rational alternative. Then we simply need to accept it. Like it or not, there is no other way. When we reach bedrock, it is time to assume solidity and start building.

Of course, we can choose to fold our arms, dig in our heels, and refuse to accept bedrock as solid. We can insist on empirical proof even at the basic foundation of our beliefs, where no such proof is available. A builder can blast a hole in the bedrock he intends to build on to see just how sturdy and dependable it really is, but then he ruins it as a basis for his foundation and must dig down even further to another stratum of rock. If he consistently questions and blasts each layer of rock he uncovers, he will never have a house; he will have just a hole in the ground. In the same way, if you refuse to accept an ultimate absolute, you will never be certain of your beliefs; you will have a hole in your life—empty and meaningless.

Please don't jump to the conclusion that we are promoting a doctrine of blind faith that ignores facts and scoffs at reason. You will see as you read on that we assert quite the opposite—that no belief should be accepted without the full support of hard-nosed reason. Yet reason comes to a point where it must lay aside its demand for empirical proof and turn to calculated assumption based on logical necessity. There is no alternative. Everyone assumes absolutes, even the most steadfast rationalist. If you have any belief at all—whether it is religious faith or atheistic naturalism—look deeply enough beneath it and you will find the assumption of an unproven absolute.[3]

Analysis and reason have great value, and we should exercise them continually and carefully. But we must remind ourselves that the purpose of analysis is to make a subject transparent so we can see the solid truth behind it. However, if we insist on making the ultimate truth transparent, our quest is doomed to end in empty meaninglessness. As C. S. Lewis put it, "It is good that the window should be transparent, because the street or garden beyond it is opaque. How if you saw through the garden too? It's no use trying to 'see through' first principles. If you see through everything, then everything is transparent. But a wholly transparent world is an invisible world. To 'see through' all things is the same as not to see."[4]

After explaining each truth by the greater truth beyond it, we will finally reach a truth that cannot be explained because there is no greater truth beyond it. This is the bedrock truth beyond all truths. It is the truth that simply must be assumed and accepted as a logical necessity with no alternative. It is the ultimate absolute for answering our deepest questions and giving meaning to everything we think and believe.

Are we saying, then, that it is impossible to know truth with certainty? If we end our quest for truth by merely assuming an unproven absolute, how can we know we are assuming the right absolute? You may assume naturalism; I may assume God. Since neither God nor naturalism can be proven by scientific methods, does this make one assumption just as good as the other? Not at all. Our empirical experience of the world provides a template that outlines the general shape of ultimate truth. We can use this template to identify the absolute that most consistently explains the reality we experience. Just as expert animal trackers can determine the species, size, and speed of a creature by reading its footprints, we can determine much about the absolute behind reality by its imprint in our world. We must make an assumption about the ultimate absolute, but not a blind assumption. Nature and our experience of reality provide more than enough evidence to justify a safe and confident assurance that truth is real and an ultimate absolute stands behind it.

Most people understand that if an ultimate absolute exists, it can be nothing short of God. But in today's world, so many people have been brought up in an environment shaped by scientific naturalism and diffused by postmodernism that God is not too obvious to question. They either doubt his existence or totally deny it. But without God as the bedrock absolute, all possibility of objective truth collapses. Those who deny God must resign themselves to believing in an accidental, mechanistic universe devoid of truth, meaning, destiny, or purpose; or they must accept a world of illusion and uncertainty about reality itself.

The purpose of this book is to display the end result of denying God's existence and to contrast it with the rational choice of affirming God as the bedrock of truth and reality. While we will not try to prove God scientifically or empirically, we will lead you to see that belief in him is a logical necessity. Either he exists or nothing in this universe makes any sense at all. God is beyond scientific proof but not beyond the proof of rational thinking. We will infer God's existence in the same way that physicists infer the existence of black holes. Black holes are by nature invisible, but astronomers know they exist because of gravitational effects on certain stars that only something like a black hole could cause. God is invisible, but we know he exists because of effects in the universe that only something like a god could cause. In that sense, we do indeed have proof of God's existence. We will show you how to affirm his existence as the ultimate absolute, so you can build on his bedrock a life of certainty.

QUESTIONS FOR THOUGHT AND DISCUSSION

1. What is an absolute?
2. What is the difference between conditional standards, natural standards, and an ultimate absolute?
3. What practical functions do standards serve in our world?
4. What is the function of an ultimate absolute?
5. Do abstractions such as truth, beauty, goodness, and love need an absolute? Why or why not?
6. Does assuming an absolute necessitate discarding reason? Explain.
7. What are the two options most people consider for the ultimate absolute? Can either of these options be proven? Why or why not?

CHAPTER THREE

CAN I TRUST
WHAT I THINK?

THE ABSOLUTE FOR REASON

The newborn baby looks up at her mother and tries to focus on the face smiling down on her. The baby has never seen a face before and has no idea what she is looking at. At first the eyes, nose, and smiling mouth mean nothing to her. She sees nothing more than masses of moving color as meaningless to her as a Jackson Pollack painting is to many of us. Even when the baby comes to understand the meaning of what she sees, her undeveloped brain will not hold the concept that the faces of her mother and father exist even when they are not within her field of vision. But later as her father begins to hide his face behind a blanket and play peek-a-boo, very quickly the connections in her brain come together and rudimentary reason begins to operate. It tells her that the face of her father exists even when she cannot see it.

As she grows, she learns to apply reason to her broadening world. For example, she has been taught that the earth is round, even though it may look flat all about her. She observes facts such as sunrises and sunsets, the disappearance of ships over the edge of the horizon, and the position of certain stars at certain times. Applying reason to these facts allows her to determine the true shape of the earth. When she touches a hot stove and reacts with pain, then sees another person doing the same thing, she reasons that all humans have certain common feelings and experiences. Reason points her toward facts and truths that she cannot know except by exercising the rational facilities of her mind.

Most of us take reason for granted. We use it every day to understand the facts about our world, facts that may not be immediately apparent to the senses. But is reason dependable? Can we believe what it tells us about facts and truths that are not readily apparent, or do our personal experiences and conditioning so overwhelm reason as to render it untrustworthy? In today's climate of uncertainty, many people are quite skeptical about the ability of reason to lead us to truth.

One of the first thinkers to address this question was the seventeenth-century French philosopher René Descartes. "I think, therefore I am," he asserted, claiming that his ability to question his existence was actually a proof of it. We sometimes wonder at the tendency of philosophers to formulate such propositions that seem to complicate facts too obvious to question. Wasn't his mirror enough to prove he existed? But Descartes's quest makes more sense than may appear at first blush. No belief is beyond question unless it rests on a solid absolute, and he was searching for some kind of solid ground to prove that existence was not an illusion. Descartes started the ball of reason rolling in modern philosophy. In seeking to prove that he existed objectively and was not just a figment in a dream, he concluded that the experience of independent thought proved his own existence in such a way that he could not doubt it.

Philosophers since Descartes have affirmed the power of the rational mind to determine not only the reality of self but also the nature of all reality. Only with the advent of postmodernism has the validity of reason been called into question. Right at the outset of our quest for truth, we must address this question. Here is why. We understand that many of our readers have an innate distrust of Scripture and religion, while others have the same distrust of science. Therefore, though we believe in the validity of both Scripture and science, we intend to avoid depending on either in making our case. Instead, we want to appeal primarily to the more common ground of reason. However, we realize the difficulty in this approach as well. Since reason now also has its detractors, we can't turn to reason unless we first show that reason is valid. We must show that it is rooted firmly in a dependable absolute, or we cannot depend on it to lead us in our quest for certainty.

THE POSTMODERN DISTRUST OF REASON

We have inherited from the Enlightenment a view of reason that has shaped the very way the Western world has thought until the middle of the twentieth century. Enlightenment philosophers believed that reason was supreme; that mankind, by the power of reason alone, could come to know all truth. The Enlightenment failed in the aftermath of the French Revolution, but it left a legacy of confidence in the power of reason, a confidence that has only recently been challenged.

In the eyes of the postmodernists, the failure of the Enlightenment has largely discredited reason. They are convinced that those who continue to depend on reason as a guide to truth are looking at reality through a lens clouded by a failed philosophy. We are fooling ourselves, they argue, to believe we are capable of thinking objectively. They tell us that we cannot trust human reason because it is hopelessly skewed by our cultural viewpoints and philosophies. They say that what we call reason is really a conditioned worldview riddled with presuppositions, biases, and lack of information. Although we claim to evaluate reality by objective reason, they say we are really evaluating it by a humanly contrived, faith-dependent philosophy of reason that we have been conditioned all our lives to *think* is objective.

In rejecting the Enlightenment's excessive claims for reason, postmodernists have swung the pendulum to the opposite extreme. It is an overstatement to say that conditioning and biases contaminate reason so severely as to disable it. Certainly none of us can escape presuppositions and biases, but does this mean we cannot know objective truth, even dimly and imperfectly, despite them? Conditioning and biases cloud the lens of reason but not to the point of shutting out light altogether. We know this to be true from our own experience. We overcome biases every time we change our minds. And sometimes we even overcome them enough to change our worldviews. If we were hopelessly stuck in the ruts of our pre-conditioned biases, all attempts at teaching and persuasion would be futile, all arguments absurd, all attempts at correction a waste of energy, and the quest for truth a game of blind man's bluff.

Postmodernists like to use the well-known illustration of blind men describing an elephant to show that reason has a fatal weakness. As you may remember, the blind man who felt only the elephant's tail reasoned that elephants were like ropes. The one who felt only its side claimed they were like walls. The one who touched its legs insisted that elephants were like trees. Each man established a premise and formed a conclusion based on the evidence at hand, but the individual conclusions did not give the men the full truth about elephants. According to postmodernists, this story shows that reason is not a dependable tool for apprehending truth.

But the failure of the blind men was not a failure of *reason;* it was a failure of *reasoning.* What the men postulated about elephants would have been true enough had their claims been more modest. The elephant's *tail*—not the entire elephant—is like a rope, its *side* is like a wall, and its *legs* are like trees. Each man described the limited part of reality that he encountered accurately enough. Their mistake was in drawing conclusions too broad to be supported by such limited data. Each tried to infer the entire elephant from an insufficient sampling of evidence. The men applied reason poorly and got poor results.

Reason is not discredited by poor usage any more than Beethoven's music is discredited by poor performances. Because distortions and misuses of reason can lead to false conclusions, postmodernists no longer want to trust reason at all as a guide to truth. The veteran watchdog sometimes barks at the wrong things, so the owners muzzle it where it can't bark at all, leaving the gate of gullibility unguarded.

Each blind man did indeed find a valid truth about the elephant, though it differed from the truths discovered by his peers. The problem was simply that none of these individual truths was the whole truth. But the limitations of personal reasoning and experience need not have kept these men from knowing more of the truth than they discovered for themselves. They could have communicated with each other, shared their experiences, and even changed places with each other, and their combined knowledge could easily have brought them quite close to the objective truth about the shape of an elephant.

But let's go a step further. What if the personal biases of one of the blind men caused him to experience even his limited samplings of the elephant in a highly subjective way, as postmodernists believe it does? Let's say that the blind man who felt the elephant's side came to the experiment heavily conditioned by his environment. Perhaps he had lived his entire life in an eccentrically decorated home where all the walls were covered with shag carpet. Heavily conditioned to believe that all vertical surfaces were always covered with shag carpet, his mind may have played a trick on him and interpreted the sensory data from his fingers to accord with what he had long been conditioned to believe rather than what his fingers actually felt. He may have sincerely believed and reported to the others that the side of an elephant is like a shag carpet. If his highly conditioned subjectivity forced him to interpret the side of the elephant in such a personal way, does that mean that his account of the side of an elephant is valid? If we say that "an elephant is like a shag carpet" is true for him, does that make it true in any meaningful way? If we allow assertions shaped by such strong personal biases, conditioning, and preconceptions to wear the label "truth," it means that the term has no real content. If everyone's truth is equally valid, then truth is a meaningless term. A word that can mean anything really means nothing. And this is close to what the postmodern mind-set is telling us about the term *truth*.

Let's go yet another step further and say that every blind man felt the elephant's side, and each had such strong preconditioned biases that the reports varied wildly. One said it felt like a stone wall, another like a plastic bag, another like the bark of a tree, and yet another like peanut butter. Although none of these highly subjective reports would help anyone understand the truth about an elephant, none would affect the true reality of the animal. The elephant would exist objectively with textures and features that retained their specific character regardless of all reports to the contrary. Truth exists objectively even if no one apprehends it accurately. Denying or ignoring this fact is at the core of the postmodern error.

There is no need to limit our knowledge solely to what we can learn within the confines of our own subjective experience. Just as the blind men could have learned more of the truth of an elephant by comparing notes, we can share data, test conclusions, and thus expand our own knowledge. We can be taught. When collective experience and applied reason indicate the general shape of truth, we can get a fair idea of the bigger picture, even though it may not always be in sharp focus.

Many people who have adopted the postmodern outlook nevertheless believe in God. They seem to accept the idea of God intuitively without feeling any need for rational proofs. But even when believers don't require verification, the capacity to verify must be there. It's like a parachute or a fire extinguisher or a spare tire. You may never expect to use it, but you need to keep it handy. Belief in God must be rational even when reason is not actively engaged. Believers need to be ready to defend its rationality because others out there do need to be convinced. For them, all unverified assertions or faith stories will seem like superstitious fables unless we can show them that our belief has a solid rational base.

Since we can't show that belief is rational to a mind that doesn't trust reason, we've first got to tackle the task of showing that reason is dependable.

Is Reason Dependable?

In the previous chapter, we asserted that everyone—both naturalists and believers—must assume and accept a bedrock absolute for what they believe to be true. Yet people set in a strict rationalist viewpoint insist that we should never assume anything. They claim we should reach all our conclusions by reason alone. But the moment they make such a claim, they also make an assumption: they assume that reason is dependable. This assumption is unavoidable because none of us can think rationally unless we do assume that reason is dependable. We question, deduce, explain, and prove all we know by the exercise of reason, but we don't question, deduce, explain, or prove the validity of reason. We simply go on reasoning and take our ability to do it for granted.

The need to question reason hardly occurs to most of us. Our thinking seems rational enough, and it seems to conform to the reality we experience. Mathematics, for example, which requires abstract reasoning, can be apparently verified by actual experience in the tangible world. We don't have to depend solely on the internal workings of our minds to know that two plus two must equal four. We can become philosophers and verify the obvious with an experiment. We can place two oranges on the table, count them carefully, and then place two more beside them and count again. Then we confirm with our senses what we reasoned abstractly in our minds—that just as we expected, we have four oranges. Abstract reasoning and experiential reality seem to coincide.

But the question remains, how do we know that either our internal thinking or the reality we perceive is objective and rational? How do we know the oranges are real or that mathematics is anything more than a trick of our brains? The thinking of a lunatic seems utterly rational to him. His experience of external reality also conforms to his internal thinking. The man who thinks he is Napoleon finds his belief confirmed irrefutably in every word, every event, every circumstance of his existence. Strike up a friendly conversation about the weather, and he may suspect you of being a spy in the service of

General Wellington trying to trick him into revealing whether he is planning an attack if it doesn't rain. A lunatic interprets reality through the filter of his delusion. He sees his world through the warped lens of his disordered mind and has no clue that his view is far from absolutely true and objective.

Even the mind of generally sane people can be subject to distortions they cannot perceive, sometimes because of influences of the moment and sometimes because of more or less permanent preconditioning and ongoing influences. I remember hearing a story that showed how temporary influences can sometimes skew reason. A man was sure that each time he went under anesthetizing gas in the dentist's chair, he thought up exceptionally creative and insightful ideas that never occurred to him in his normal mode of thinking. But when he emerged from the influence of the gas, he was frustrated that he could never remember any of these gems of wisdom. On his next trip to the dentist he carried a pencil and pad to record these insights as he thought them. When the effects of the gas wore off, he looked at his pad and found that he had written, "Higgamus-piggamus, men are all bigamous, Hoggamus-poggamus, women are monogamous."

Obviously the dentist's gas completely addled the man's rationality, but it also skewed his judgment so much that he was in no condition to know it. For all we know, we are in the same boat unless we can find an absolute for reason more solid than our own subjective intuition that it just seems to work. Without such an absolute we have no way of knowing whether we are thinking rational thoughts about a rational universe, or whether we are all lunatics in an asylum where every thought is an illusion that seems rational only to ourselves.

Does reason have such an absolute? Is there any way we can

know that we are any different from those who insist that they are the reincarnation of Napoleon?

When we try to prove absolutely the validity of reason, we find ourselves facing a strange dilemma. As C. S. Lewis pointed out, it is impossible to prove that human reason is dependable because we must use human reason to prove it. If you question reason, you can't trust your own reasoning processes to affirm its validity. When reason is in question, its own claim to be valid is meaningless. We can't expect reason to testify against itself. When the judge is also the accused, the verdict is surely suspect. So we have a dilemma on our hands. We cannot prove the reliability of reason, yet if we are uncertain about reason, we must be uncertain about our capacity to know any truth at all.

We would guess that very few of us waste brainpower trying to prove that reason is dependable. We simply go on reasoning and take the results for granted. We tend to assume reason as being foundational—one of those givens that, until lately, no one has seriously questioned.

However, before we allow ourselves to assume that reason is valid because it is foundational, we need to look at the foundation. If we are to trust the dependability of reason, we must be sure that it has the undergirding support of a solid absolute. In the postmodern view, reason is suspect because postmodernists cannot be sure of such an absolute. Unless we can find this absolute, we are left to face that dilemma that Lewis posed in which reason has no validating authority but itself.

THE DILEMMA OF THE NATURALIST

Those who believe in a naturalistic universe claim that everything came into being without the activity of an external, supernatural first cause. Naturalists believe that random combinations of atoms just happened to bump into each other and stick together to form everything that exists. For naturalists, this view is the only possible explanation for the existence of the universe. Such a view cannot validate reason because when things collide and combine at random, the results must be considered irrational, meaning without reason. Therefore, a universe that grew accidentally out of random forces is by definition a universe without reason. According to this model of origins, the human brain—the only reasoning organ we know of—is a product of these same random, accidental forces. Naturalists see the brain as nothing more than a chance cluster of molecules thrown together by the random movements of irrational forces.

So how can naturalists trust such a mind to reach rational conclusions about reality? Their affirmation of reason is highly suspect because irrational causes cannot be trusted to produce rational results. Rational thinking forces us to conclude that the universe cannot produce anything greater than the sum total of all that exists within it. In other words, if reason did not exist in the universe at the outset, it cannot magically poof itself into existence in the course of the universe's development. To claim otherwise is to put oneself in the position of medieval alchemists who thought they could turn lead into gold. An irrationally produced, chaotic, materialistic universe does not contain the kind of stuff reason is made of, so how can we assume that it could produce a mind capable of rendering a rational explanation about reality and truth? We can't. We can no more expect a mind produced by a mindless universe to explain reality and truth than we can expect stirring a bowl of alphabet soup to produce a Shakespearean sonnet or even a sentence from a first-grade reader.

Many naturalists with a postmodern bent have accepted this conclusion—that the universe is irrational and all our thinking is undependable. Others are still trying to have their cake and eat it too. They believe that the universe manifests order, reason, and objective reality in spite of its random and accidental origins. But as we have shown above, such a view is self-contradictory. People can hold it only if they have not thought out the problem to its obvious conclusion. They are like the cartoon character who unwittingly walks off a cliff into thin air but does not fall until he looks down and realizes he is not supported. Naturalists who think reason is rational in spite of its random origins have walked off a cliff into irrationality, but they don't realize it. They think they are walking on the solid ground of reason, but there is nothing but air beneath them. If they continue to apply reason in defending their beliefs, the inconsistency of it will sooner or later break the surface. At that point they will either admit the inadequacy of their position and change it, or they will deny reason in order to maintain it.

A naturalistic universe simply cannot supply from within itself a validation for the dependability of reason. Such a universe and everything in it must be considered accidental, random, and irrational, continually in a state of flux, change, and unpredictability. In such a universe there is no bedrock, no solid footing to support human reason. Unless the lever of reason rests solidly on a fulcrum that is firm and unmoving, we cannot use reason to pry the lid off of truth and find certainty. Reason must have its origin in a rational absolute that exists outside and above the natural universe or our claim to be rational creatures is not credible.

THE BEDROCK FOR REASON

We do not make the Enlightenment claim that reason can encompass all truth. But we do claim that all truth is rational and that adopting a belief that contradicts clear facts or plain reason is irrational. Contradictory claims cannot both be true.

We readily concede that some realities are beyond the reach of reason, and we must not deny their existence simply because we lack data on them. It is not irrational to adopt a belief whose claims go beyond our understanding as long as those claims do not contradict reason. For example, you may believe in the existence of spirits even though you can neither collect hard data on them nor comprehend their mode of being. Such a belief is not inherently irrational because while we may never directly see, touch, or hear spirits, nothing in our experience of reality contradicts their possible existence. Reason may not be able to encompass it, but reason cannot refute it.

But we cannot believe in an outright contradiction. For example, we cannot believe in the simultaneous existence of both an immovable object and an irresistible force because if these two objects were to meet, one or the other—if not both—would be proved false. Two objects thus labeled cannot exist mutually within the same universe. They are contradictory, and to believe in both is irrational. We cannot synthesize opposites into a rational belief. We must choose one option as true and reject the other. Or where data is insufficient, we must simply suspend judgment.

The need to square faith with reason is real. In chapter 8 we will explore the relationship of faith and reason more thoroughly, but suffice it to say at this point that our faith must be consistent with reason. British journalist and author G. K. Chesterton has his amateur detective priest Father Brown explaining to a criminal who had impersonated a priest how he knew the man was not a real cleric. "You attacked reason," said Father Brown. "It's bad theology."[1] Faith and reason are children of the same father. Reason provides a vital platform for faith to stand on as it peers over the edge of the empirical world in search of the ultimate absolute.

No one should be content to leave the question of the validity of reason unanswered because the search for absolute truth depends on it. And the search for truth is not a trivial pursuit or a mere intellectual exercise; it is of vital importance because of what is riding on the outcome. It is perilous to turn aside from the question. If we find that absolute truth exists, many other things unbelievers might prefer to shut out may exist as well. As we asserted in chapter 2, the existence of absolute truth means the existence of a supernatural creator of the universe. And if such a creator exists, his claims on his creatures are enormously important realities that we must come to grips with. We must doggedly pursue the answers to these questions or face the possibility of immeasurable consequences. And reason is necessary as a guide in that search. That is why the validity of reason is a question of vital importance.

Finding the bedrock absolute to validate reason involves an assumption, but it's an unavoidable assumption that squares with both experience and logic. We must assume that a reasoning mind must be the product of a superior reasoning mind. Reason could not have arisen from within the natural universe because nature, before humans came on the scene, was mindless and devoid of the stuff reason is made of. Therefore, reason must have originated from a supernatural source, or, to go straight to the bottom line, from God. This assumption traces reason to a solid, rational source outside the natural universe. With its source being superior to the natural universe, reason is in a position to make judgments about the universe—about facts and truth and reality—that we can safely depend on as accurate.

Embracing God as the source of reason solves the logical dilemma of reason's existence and gives it an absolute that guarantees its trustworthiness. You can reject this conclusion, of course, just as you can reject belief in spirits on the basis of insufficient empirical data. But reason does not deserve such a rejection because, while the data on God is not of the sort that lends itself to scientific proof, nothing about believing in God contradicts reason or our experience of reality. If you reject God as reason's ultimate absolute, you have nowhere else to turn. Deny God as the source and absolute for reason, and you leave reason afloat in a sea of irrationality. Your alternative to God is to live in a world of uncertainty about what is real and true.

It boils down to this: If you trust reason, you must believe in God. If you don't believe in God, you can't trust reason. Remove God as reason's absolute, and you pull the rug out from under the belief that we are rational beings. When reason collapses, our certainty of any truth falls with it. To put it simply, either you believe in God or you cannot be sure there is anything to believe in at all.

QUESTIONS FOR THOUGHT AND DISCUSSION

1. Can all truth be reached by reason? Why or why not?
2. How can we know that reason is dependable?
3. Why can't reason validate its own dependability?
4. Could random forces have produced reason? Explain.
5. Can experience, worldviews, and environment undermine reason's dependability? Why or why not?
6. Why does reason need an absolute outside nature to be valid?
7. If God is not the source of reason, can reason validate truth? Explain.

CHAPTER FOUR

WHO DECIDES WHAT IS RIGHT?

THE ABSOLUTE FOR MORALITY

At lunch Mark and a coworker decided to try out a new restaurant across town. As he drove down the freeway, a Chevy Suburban suddenly changed lanes and whipped into the tight space in front of him, causing him to slam on his brakes.

"Come on!" Mark yelled as he leaned on his horn. "You turkey!"

After another mile or so, he glanced in his rearview mirror to see an eighteen wheeler bearing down on him until it was only a few short feet from his rear bumper.

"You idiot!" he cried. "Do you think you own the freeway and the rest of us should pull off and bow as you go by?"

As Mark pulled into the restaurant parking lot, he spotted a space just vacated not far from the door. He was about to turn into the slot when a girl in a little Ford Escort zoomed toward him from the other direction. As he stopped to avoid a collision, the girl whipped into the parking space.

"Of all the nerve!" Mark cried. "Couldn't she see that we were about to pull into that space?"

Outrage from drivers like Mark is not at all uncommon. We've all seen it happen. Most of us have expressed such outrage ourselves.

These tirades show us that everyone has an innate sense of right and wrong. We all generally expect to be treated fairly and courteously. We assume that those around us know the basic common rules of right behavior, and we believe they should conform to them. Some people deny that such rules exist, and all of us occasionally ignore the rules or break them. But our behavior shows clearly that deep down inside, we all have an innate sense of morality. People would not yell at rude drivers unless they believed that rude driving is wrong. It makes no sense to express anger at bad behavior unless you believe there is a standard that defines good behavior. And you assume that everyone out there is aware of this standard. In fact, before you can disagree with anyone about anything, the two of you must agree on one thing: a standard of right and wrong. Adversaries in an argument must assume they share a common standard that defines right before either can expect to convince the other that a standard has been violated.

We all take morality for granted. It is something that everyone assumes to be universally true. We treat it as an absolute. This universal moral sense is another telling landmark in our search for certainty.

THE UNIVERSAL NATURE OF MORALITY

We find a sense of morality in every society around the world, from the most primitive to the most advanced. We find it in the records of all past cultures as well as in all present cultures. And the morality of all these societies is surprisingly similar, no matter how widely separated by time, geography, cultural development, or religious belief. The morality defined in the Jewish Ten Commandments, the Babylonian Code of Hammurabi, the Chinese Tao, and the Christian New Testament differ in detail and emphasis but not in essence. Some societies allow individuals to kill to avenge a wrong, while others insist that all execution is the prerogative of the state. Some societies allow freedom in premarital sexual relationships or permit men to take more than one wife, while others forbid such behavior. But all have rules that say people cannot kill others at will or engage in sex with just anyone they want. All have laws protecting human life, all have rules governing marriage and family relationships, all condemn stealing, and all encourage doing good to others.

Some societies enforce morality strictly, while others are lax on one or more points. And within every society there are people who resist the imposition of morality on their behavior. When a significant number of such people gain power or support for their position, significant aberrations to the universal moral sense can occur, as it did in Hitler's Germany or in the acceptance of killing female babies in some Asian countries. Usually these aberrations are short-lived, as elements within or outside a society will become outraged enough to rise up and stop the aberrant behavior. But despite such variations and distortions, the same basic sense of morality appears wherever humans live together. It's as if many different orchestras are playing from the same score but adapting the harmonics to fit their own instruments.

How can we explain a moral code that is so consistently present in all societies? How do we explain a sense of morality that gives virtually every sane person on the planet an innate sense of right and wrong? Why should such a moral sense exist at all? Believers explain it easily: God planted the standards of morality in the human conscience and stands as the ultimate absolute behind it. This explanation shows us why the moral code is universal and also gives it the weight of authority.

Obviously, unbelievers deny that morality must derive from God. But without God as the source, any rational explanation for morality collapses. As prominent ethicist Richard Taylor says, "The modern age, more or less repudiating the idea of a divine lawgiver, has nevertheless tried to retain the ideas of moral right and wrong, not noticing that, in casting God aside, they have also abolished the conditions of meaningfulness for moral right and wrong as well. Thus, even educated persons sometimes declare that such things as war, or abortion, or the violation of certain human rights, are 'morally wrong,' and they imagine that they have said something true and significant. Educated people do not need to be told, however, that questions such as these have never been answered outside of religion."[1]

Without God as the source and basis of morality, we cannot find an explanation for it that is consistent with reality. However, a number of alternative theories have been advanced. We will look at these theories and demonstrate why they do not stand up to scrutiny.

THE INVENTION THEORY OF MORALITY

The invention theory explains morality as a set of rules that humans have devised for self-preservation through trial and error over the millennia of history. According to this theory, nothing is absolute about these rules. They were not handed down by some mountaintop god but grew out of humanity's own common sense and practical thinking. The idea behind moral behavior is not conformity to some overarching truth, but simple survival. The theory says the rules we call morality are simply the guidelines we have found to work in a society huddled together for mutual protection against a hostile universe. Behavior that helped or strengthened society was encouraged and called "right." Behavior that hurt or weakened it was prohibited and called "wrong." According to the invention theory, society forms governments to determine the exact shape of the morality that will best preserve it, and the government expresses the moral will of the people by passing laws to enforce the standards for belief and behavior.

But we find a major flaw in the invention theory. Whenever people try to determine right for themselves, they always start by assuming that something is already intrinsically right. When people claim that morality is simply mankind's invention to preserve society, they assume that society ought to be preserved. It is the assumed, unproven truth on which their morality rests. They may deny that absolutes for morality exist, but the moment they make any kind of moral claim—such as the proposition that society ought to be preserved—they have planted their feet on a moral absolute. They can't help but do so because for any foundational assumption to be held as valid, it must be based on an absolute. Unbelievers may lock the door against absolutes of any kind, but the moment they claim any action to be right or wrong, some kind of absolute has sneaked in through the window.

The assumption that society ought to be preserved may be another of those tenets that seem too obvious to question. But is it really? Isolate the idea from God, and it can be neither proven nor supported by reason. From the unbelievers' point of view, it is not even a reasonable idea. They have only a few short years to call their own, and then it's all over for them. Why should they care if civilization survives past their own death? They have no stake in its future. Why should they divert precious time and energy from their own brief lives to do anything for others? And yet unbelievers do so the world over.

People who do not believe in God may claim that they look out for others because they think it is the unselfish, right, and noble thing to do. They may even be sincere when they say this because these innate feelings come from their hearts. But it makes no sense for such feelings to be in their hearts. The feelings are inconsistent with their denial of God. Terms like *unselfishness, sacrifice, nobility,* and *concern for others* have no real meaning without a solid absolute on which to base them. Without absolutes to prescribe such unselfish behavior, it makes perfect sense for unbelievers to spend every precious moment packing their own lives with all the pleasure and gratification they can grab, and let society take care of its own future.

But in spite of what makes sense, all of us—believers and unbelievers alike—are saddled with the notion that there are certain things all humans ought to do. We ought to give aid to those in need. We ought to defend innocent children against abuse. We ought to be honest and truthful. No one, not even unbelievers, can break free from the tug of such "oughts." They grip us like gravity. When we look beneath these oughts, we find the assumed absolute: Society ought to be preserved. That idea should mean nothing to unbelievers, yet they can't get rid of it. It's like trying to throw away a boomerang—it keeps coming back. The concept is firmly entrenched in the mind of every sane human being, yet human reason did not produce it and cannot defend it.

Here is the dilemma of unbelievers: Since they cannot prove by reason that society ought to be preserved, they must choose between two alternatives—they must either accept the idea as an absolute or reject it as an outrageous demand in a godless universe where self is on its own. If they accept it as an absolute, they lose their rationale for being unbelievers because such a counterintuitive moral concept can have force only if it has roots in an absolute God to whom we are responsible. But if unbelievers reject God as the authority behind morality, they must dismiss the tug of their hearts toward duty to others as an illusion. Of course, even if they dismiss it, they may still choose to give in to it—not because they think it right or wrong, but merely because doing good to others makes them feel good. If the preservation of society is an absolute truth from God, then the laws we pass to curb the impulses of individuals for the benefit of the whole have force. But if the preservation of society is merely a human concept, there is nothing absolute about these laws and they are unfair because they contradict the rights of the individual.

If there is no transcendent God, there can be no such thing as true and absolute right. If there is no God, we cannot condemn people for dedicating their lives to their own pleasure and we cannot demand that they place society above themselves. We have no standard by which we can prove that doing good to others is any better than ignoring the needs of others and doing good only for oneself. In such a world it would be futile for Mark to express outrage at the girl who stole the parking place. She was just doing what seemed best for herself at the moment. In a world without God to underscore absolutes, we can't expect anyone to drive or live according to any standard society chooses to set up. If there is no God, all rules are mere opinion and none have authority. If there is no God to give mankind a hope for life after death, you may as well ignore any notions of rightness that self-appointed moralists shove at you and get on with the business of doing only what you want. As Russian novelist Fyodor Dostoyevsky said: "If there is no immortality of the soul, there can be no virtue and therefore everything is permissible."[2] Let's be up front and admit it: a world in which "anything is permissible" has a certain surface appeal. We all hide within us an impulse to kick aside the rules, flex our freedom, ignore the expectations of law, and do just what we want to do. But it won't work. Life without rules and authority becomes a maze of traps and disasters because when we remove the restriction of law, we also remove its protection. Without law we can never expect to be treated fairly or safely because society's capacity to protect life and property evaporates. Stable relationships become impossible. Families disintegrate. Murder, rape, and theft become rampant. Order decays into anarchy, and life must be lived in the unstable, uncertain environment of the lawless jungle. Theologian and philosopher William Lane Craig writes that, "One Rabbi who was imprisoned at Auschwitz said that it was as though all the Ten Commandments had been reversed: thou shalt kill, thou shalt lie, thou shalt steal. Mankind has never seen such a hell. And yet, in a real sense, if naturalism is true, our world is Auschwitz. There is no good and evil, no right and wrong. Objective moral values do not exist."[3]

Whether God exists is not merely a theoretical abstraction that has no practical bearing on our everyday lives. When belief in God wanes and dies, society loses its stable underpinnings and spins downward into a maelstrom of fragmented individualism with each person out for his or her own gain and each of us the potential victim of all the others.

THE SOCIAL CONTRACT THEORY OF MORALITY

Some unbelievers may say, "We agree that life in society would be disastrous without laws. We need laws to put reasonable limits on the potentially intrusive behavior of others so we can get on with the business of doing our own thing. But these laws need not be based on the authority of God or an external absolute. Law works just fine as a social contract among individuals in society. We all mutually agree to give up a little freedom so that all can enjoy a reasonable amount of freedom. We determine our morality not by some overarching absolute standard of right and wrong but by the consensus of society. By common agreement, everyone accepts the morality expressed by the will of the majority."

This second theory, the social contract theory, contains two flaws, both deadly. First, if morality is simply what the majority of society legislates and nothing more, why should the minority follow it? We can find no rational basis for asking the minority to accept the social contract—to give up its wants and bend to the will of the majority. What does the consensus of numbers have to do with my personal desires? As a member of the minority, I may follow the will of the majority as long as I find it convenient. I may even follow it generally because I realize the value of it. I may sacrifice some of my personal wants to preserve social stability because I have the good sense to see that I benefit in the long run. But I will follow law only to the extent that it does benefit me or up to the limits the government can enforce. People who believe law to be without absolute moral authority will not take obedience seriously. They will obey it only when it helps them to accomplish their own ends or when the risk of getting caught is too great.

If there is no God, this indifferent approach to law is perfectly reasonable—but utterly fatal. The refusal to recognize God as the absolute authority behind right and wrong will eventually cause society to destroy itself. We can see the beginnings of such disintegration in the United States as the recognition of God is increasingly pushed out of public life. The Founding Fathers understood that the law by which nations should be governed was more than a mere social contract. The Declaration of Independence explicitly recognized God as the absolute behind law when it proposed separation from England in order to assume "the separate and equal station to which the Laws of Nature and of Nature's God entitle them." But now that God is being pushed out as the absolute behind law, we see the authority of our nation's constitution disintegrating. The courts seem determined to accede to individuals bent on destroying any overarching law that stands between them and full satisfaction of their own cravings. With no allegiance to God, people will increasingly chip away at the restriction of law to gain more and more freedom to follow their wants and urges. The ability of law to restrain these urges will wear down, and individuals will come to have little or no allegiance to society as a whole. All their attention will be focused on themselves—their own rights, wants, and pleasures. Without the pressure of a true and absolute morality, people will lose all motivation to sacrifice personal satisfaction for duty to others.

The second fatal flaw of the social contract theory is this: When society begins to disintegrate into self-centered individualism, the population becomes vulnerable to the tyranny of what philosopher Friedrich Nietzsche called "the will to power." A disintegrating society adrift with no bedrock of morality will be at the mercy of those in power, who, with no true guide to right and wrong, will impose their own will on the rest. It is the "might makes right" concept. Right will be solely what those who wield the power want it to be.

When people ignore traditional morality and seize power to serve their own ends, the results can be hideous. Adolph Hitler's demonic rule over Germany in the late 1930s and early 1940s is a sobering example. Hitler dreamed of a Germanic people purified and enthroned as the master race of the world. Obsessed with his dream, he ignored any moral principle that stood in his way and made his own rules for his own benefit. He readily stripped his victims of property, freedom, dignity, justice, and even their lives in order to rid the world of races he thought inferior to his own.

We see something similar happening in America today as the concept of an overarching, true morality begins to crumble. In the name of personal freedom, those in power have legislated the right to kill the unborn simply because having a child would inconvenience the lifestyle of the parents. Such a law flouts traditional morality. It is a raw example of those in power destroying those with no power to resist. The strong victimizing the weak is the ultimate result when society thinks it can legislate morality to fit its own whims. But the people who benefit from such laws today may become its victims tomorrow when they are the ones deemed expendable by those who wield the power.

Society cannot survive its attempts to make its own morality. When we try to determine right for ourselves, we become guided solely by our immediate needs or wants. We lack the wisdom to see the long-term result of our choices. When we take it into our own hands to decide what is right and wrong, we are like a bug on the floor so desperately seeking shelter that it runs for cover into the trap of the exterminator.

The universal, worldwide moral code does not take into account our immediate urges. We may want our neighbor's car or bank account or wife, but that moral code says we can't have it. We may think a little white lie would enhance our reputation, but that old morality says we can't tell it. The moral code concerns itself not with our immediate wants but with our long-term good. To see beyond the satisfaction of our immediate impulses takes more knowledge of the workings of the human organism than any human has. True morality embodies that knowledge because it comes from the God who created humankind and knows the inner workings of the human heart.

THE INSTINCT THEORY OF MORALITY

Some unbelievers assert that rather than being a social invention, the universal moral code is instinctual. According to this third theory, the instinct theory, we humans have a concept of right and wrong because nature gave it to us. Evolution weeded out all the unworkable formulas, they say, leaving us with a conscience genetically programmed with moral instincts for preserving the race. The moral urges we all experience are simply nature's way of spurring us toward self-preserving behavior. Whenever we behave morally, we are merely obeying nature.

But the instinct theory also is flawed. Before we can obey nature, we must ask which nature we should obey. We often have conflicting urges. Sometimes we have the urge to satisfy all our wants, pursue pleasure, and gratify self. At other times we are moved to help a stranded motorist, patiently soothe a screaming infant at two o'clock in the morning, sit up all night with a sick friend, or even sacrifice our lives for another person.

Often these conflicting urges occur simultaneously, and we must decide between them. We have all seen this dilemma pictured humorously as a person harassed by a little angel perched on one shoulder and a little demon on the other. When approaching a stranded motorist, the little angel figure urges the driver, "Pull over, and offer assistance. It's the right thing to do. Wouldn't you want someone to do the same for you?" But from the other shoulder comes the voice of the demon, "If you stop to help, you'll be late for your appointment, or you might get your clothes dirty or even get mugged. Besides, that poor slob probably wouldn't stop to help you."

It is rarely this simple or this comical, of course. Many times a day we must choose between competing urges. Shall I exercise patience with my obstinate teenager or blow my stack again? Shall I help my spouse with a household chore or zone out in front of the TV? Shall I cut my employee some slack for being late to the meeting or jump down his throat? Shall I race to the cellar as the tornado approaches or run to the neighbor's house to rescue a child left home alone?

Few people would disagree about which are the right choices in the examples above. We all admire people who put the needs of others first, and we scorn those who always put themselves first. But if nature gave us both urges, isn't it strange that we applaud one and condemn the other? By what standard do we make such a judgment? It can't be by any standard nature provides because that would have nature contradicting itself. To make a right decision between these competing urges implies a standard that exists above both. If all urges come from nature, the standard that judges between them cannot also be from nature. It must come from some source outside nature.

When we examine the motivation to save a neighbor's child in a tornado, can we truly say that there is anything natural about it? We can see why the urge to head straight for the cellar is natural; we recognize self-preservation as a basic instinct. But what is natural about risking one's brief life in a cause that cannot possibly benefit the person taking the risk? It is clear that unbelievers need to rethink the concept that the impulse to sacrifice self comes from nature. Personal sacrifice for the sake of others runs utterly against the urge of self-preservation, yet it is considered the highest of virtues by unbelievers and believers alike.

The idea that morality is an instinct given to us by nature has one big, obvious problem: If our sense of right comes from nature, why isn't it more natural? Why does morality so often prod us to act in opposition to other natural urges? We have continuing urges that lead us to go with the flow, give in to those self-serving wants and desires, protect the self at all costs, never risk anything valuable for another. But along comes another urge issuing from that mystery we call conscience—that meddlesome little angel on our right shoulder—butting in uninvited and dashing cold water on our party. It tells us not to do that thing we really want to do, not because refraining will make us any better off—indeed, it often seems to make us worse off, at least immediately—but simply because it isn't right to do it. You want to keep the twenty-dollar bill the cashier accidentally gave you in change, but that persistent voice, which you wish would hush up and go away, prods you to give it back. You would like to copy the test paper you can so easily see on your classmate's desk, but that irksome voice tells you to keep your eyes to yourself. Morality is not natural. It is too much at odds with our natural desires to share kinship with them. Morality obviously is an intruder from somewhere outside nature.

THE TRUE MEANING OF MORALITY

All of the unbelievers' explanations for morality overlook the same essential difficulty: Morality simply does not align well with human nature. The invention and social contract theories don't work because, had mankind invented the rules of right and wrong, they would have made them more compatible with natural human impulses. If you were inventing a new language, you would come up with sounds and words your tongue could pronounce easily and naturally. But morality is like a language from another galaxy. It asks us to perform in ways that are neither easy nor natural for us, the opposite of what we would expect of a human invention.

The instinct theory has the same basic problem. If morality were an instinct that evolved with the human race, right behavior would be as natural for us as it is for salmon to swim upstream to spawn and for geese to fly south for the winter. We would do right without even thinking about it. But it is neither natural nor easy for us to do what we call right. We find ourselves in continual conflict with morality, yet we can't get rid of this persistent sense of right and wrong. It's like a catchy tune we keep on humming long after we're sick of hearing it.

Who wrote that tune? If morality did not come from ourselves or from nature, where did it come from? Richard Taylor tells us that the options are limited: "Contemporary writers in ethics, who blithely discourse upon moral right and wrong and moral obligation without any reference to religion, are really just weaving intellectual webs from thin air; which amounts to saying that they discourse without meaning."[4] Dr. Taylor is right. The choice comes down to only two real possibilities: Either morality came from God, or it is an inexplicable illusion with no meaning. Of those two options, it is completely rational to accept the idea that God is the absolute for morality and that he wired us with this moral sense in order to keep our natural urges from leading us to disaster.

Why would God burden us with a morality that doesn't seem to fit us and so rudely intrudes on our wants and urges? The short answer is relationships. Morality keeps us fit for relationships and guides us in interpersonal conduct. The absolutes of right and wrong provide a template to guide you in loving your neighbor and relating to God. Morality is all about how to love effectively.

Why is it right to stop and help stranded motorists but wrong to veer over and run them down? The moral code dictates that it is right to stop because that code came from God and reflects his nature. His nature is love, and it is right to render help because such an act is the loving thing to do. The loving helpfulness that morality encourages is healthy for society. The objective standard is the ancient but timeless Golden Rule: "Do for others as you would like them to do for you."

Why do you feel a stab of conscience when you lie to your spouse, parent, child, or boss? Because deceit and distrust erode relationships, while honesty and truthfulness bond people together with trust. You feel good about telling the truth and uncomfortable about lying because truth reflects the nature of God, after whose nature the rules for right are patterned. Truthfulness is loving because it protects you from the pain of damaged relationships that results from duplicity and distrust. The same is true for all the other "oughts" and "ought nots."

Morality is like the manual for maintaining your automobile. It tells you how the car should run, gives guidance for recognizing malfunctions and instructions for repair. The whole purpose is to keep the machine running well and safely so it will take you to your destination without colliding with other automobiles. Morality serves a similar purpose for humans. It defines the properly functioning person and keeps him or her from clashing with neighbors, thus enabling relationships to flourish. When we understand the benefits of morality, its irritations become easier to bear. God desires that we live not in lonely isolation but in joyful, satisfying relationships. Morality flows to us from his own nature as our guide to maintaining and nurturing these relationships.

1. How can we explain the similarity of morality in all societies in all places at all times?
2. Why isn't it possible that morality is humanity's invention for preserving society?
3. Why is it unlikely that morality is merely a social contract reflecting the will of the majority?
4. Why is it unlikely that morality is instinctual or natural?
5. Why is it illogical for unbelievers to subscribe to any code of morality?
6. Explain Dostoyevsky's statement, "If there is no immortality of the soul, there can be no virtue and therefore everything is permissible."
7. What does morality mean to you personally and to your relationships?

CHAPTER FIVE

WHAT'S THE POINT OF IT ALL?

THE ABSOLUTE FOR MEANING

I sat across the restaurant table from a highly educated former agnostic who had just crossed the border into full belief. Remembering my own conversion, I assumed that, like most of us, this man decided to become a Christian because of the beauty of creation or the promise of heaven or perhaps the threat of judgment. But he insisted that it was none of these things.

"The thing that drew me to God," he explained, "was the sense of meaning and stability that having a God brings to the universe. It was something I had longed for all my life. I appreciate all the personal advantages that come with belief in God. But I would have believed in spite of the promise of heaven or the threat of hell; I can see that without God, the universe has no possible meaning. Without God I was adrift in a sea of 'whys' that could not be answered."

My friend was right. The search for certainty is at the same time a search for the meaning of human existence and the meaning of the universe in which we exist. When atheists, agnostics, naturalists, or unbelievers of any description take God out of the universe, everything loses its meaning. Without God, we are alone and unprotected in a dying universe that has no plan or purpose. The unbeliever may try to find momentary comfort in the theory of evolution, which gives the illusion that people are gradually improving and may eventually overcome the deficiencies in their own nature and even conquer death. But the hard truth is that the universe is running down toward ultimate oblivion, and nothing can be done to stop it. In the mind of the naturalist, the story will end in the tragedy of a lifeless universe with all energy expended, all suns dead and cold.

It is useless for unbelievers to gaze into the night sky and ask why they have been placed on this planet because without God there is no one in the endless, black silence who will even hear the question, let alone provide an answer. Without God as the ultimate absolute, there can be no why and no reason to ask for one.

A WORLD WITHOUT MEANING

Without God, mankind's existence is meaningless and the human position is hopeless. If we are not the products of a creator, we are merely accidental machines programmed with reflexes and responses that cause us to do whatever we do. Without God, freedom has no meaning, responsibility has no meaning, and goodness, heroism, justice, and love have no meaning. Neither do hate, lust, treachery, lying, or cowardice. If we are nothing more than randomly programmed machines, a person who commits murder is merely doing what a machine of a given type and programming is conditioned to do under a given set of circumstances and stimuli. How can society rightly judge or punish a machine for doing what a machine does? In a world without God, people, their ideals, and all their activities are utterly meaningless.

To the naturalists, mankind is no different from anything else that exists. In an accidental universe we are merely temporary clusters of atoms with no more importance than any other clusters, whether they be rocks, fence posts, or pill bugs. In such a view, we are nothing more than aimless lumps of matter stuck to a mass of the material we are composed of, floating in the empty void of a meaningless universe that will burn itself out as blindly as it banged itself in.

Without God, the universe offers nothing but despair. If there is no higher power to place value on humanity and give us purpose, any sense of a meaningful existence is an illusion. If you came into being accidentally with no plan and if your existence is terminal with nothing but a void of oblivion beyond, how can you muster up enough sense of purpose to get out of bed in the morning? And what does it matter how you occupy your hours, days, and years? Regardless of how important your plans and activities may seem at the moment, how can you find real meaning in them if everything you do is purposeless and destined to end in nothingness when the universe burns out and dies?

In an article on the beginnings of the universe, Rick Gore, a senior writer for *National Geographic,* wrote, "So what is the point of a universe that ends in such oblivion? The more I begin to comprehend the universe, the more that question bothers me. I have no answer, beyond some memories that will not decay."[1]

We can easily forgive Mr. Gore for tempering his despair with a little rhetorical wishful thinking, but we all know that if his view of the universe is correct, his memories *will* decay. The passing of the universe will leave nothing at all in its wake, not even a memory. Unbelievers must share Mr. Gore's despair. To them, the story of the universe is a cruel tragedy of matter bringing itself to life, waking itself to consciousness, raising itself to intelligence, and dreaming itself into eternity, only to face inevitable, unalterable, total oblivion.

It seems ironic that naturalists, pronouncing the vast realm of nature to be the sum total of reality, thought they were freeing themselves by getting rid of the oppressive idea of God. But instead they imprisoned themselves inside a dead-end universe with no way out. If God exists in an unlimited supernatural realm above nature, we have a connection to a transcendent being who gives our lives purpose. We have a doorway out of close-ended nature into an infinite realm without limits. Instead of enlarging humanity's universe, the naturalists' removal of God has shrunk it to the size of a coffin. Novelist John Updike put it plainly enough: "If this physical world is all, then it is a closed hell in which we are confined, as Pascal said elsewhere, like prisoners in chains, condemned to watch other prisoners being slain."[2]

Save yourself the trouble of exploring the many philosophies that attempt to explain existence and find meaning in it apart from God. Meaning simply cannot be found apart from him. Either God is the absolute of the universe, or the universe is meaningless. Either God is the source of moral law, or morality is an illusion. Either God is the source of reason, or everything is irrational. It's as if we are all swept downstream in a swift river and must choose between climbing onto a rock or plunging over a waterfall. One option offers security and a solid grip on stable reality; the other ends in a tumbling fall into a void where nothing has meaning and nothing is true. The choice is God or nothing; we have no other alternatives.

THE INCONSISTENCY OF UNBELIEF

When people choose unbelief over belief in God, they choose a view of the universe so out of step with reality that it is impossible to live consistently with it. The universe is too relentlessly rational and orderly to allow us to construct our own version of reality. Every day unbelievers will be forced to contend with and make decisions about realities they steadfastly deny but cannot elude.

One of these realities is the existence of a self with its attendant conscience. In a meaningless universe where people are no more than machines, there is no need or explanation for a sense of self or the moral supervision of a conscience. Unbelievers may deny that self is real, yet they must deal with an inexplicable internal presence that has all the earmarks of self. They may deny that conscience is real, but a phantom presence exactly like a conscience will prod them all the same.

In C. S. Lewis's novel *That Hideous Strength,* Professor Frost, an unbelieving social scientist, recognizes the presence of this self within his being, a presence that seems to stand above the machine he claims to be. The professor's self keeps a running commentary on all his activities and makes unwelcome judgments about his decisions and actions. Frost resents this self and denies the existence of it, insisting it is an illusion, a phantom projected by his consciousness. The ultimate horror descends on the man as he faces sudden death. In that instant he realizes that this self and its conscience were never illusions, but absolutely real.

This thing called conscience—that intrusive, uninvited voice that so often challenges our intentions—is inexplicable in a naturalistic universe. Unbelievers may try to deny its existence, but just like believers, they feel guilty when they lie or steal. They are appalled at themselves when they lose their temper and hurt a friend or a loved one. They can't stand bearing the blame for their misdeeds, so they make excuses to justify their bad behavior. Even the worst, most godless criminals always have a rationale for their crimes. They were mistreated or deprived as children; society has cheated them, and they are getting even; their victims had it coming; treating themselves to someone else's property just levels the playing field after a run of bad luck.

People who operate outside the bounds of the universal moral code always grope for traditional morality to justify their errant behavior. They saw off the limb they sit on then grab for the trunk to keep from falling. Sane people cannot live with themselves without finding some way, whether real or contrived, to justify their own behavior by the standard the universe prescribes. If the universe is really meaningless and humans are nothing more than impersonal blobs of atoms, unbelievers shouldn't need to scramble for excuses—but they do. They feel compelled to align themselves with the universal standard of morality even though they deny the existence of such a standard. Their behavior is Exhibit A of the very reality they deny. And if they fail to justify themselves, the conscience they deny will sting them just as painfully as it does believers.

Just as the existence of the eye implies light and the existence of the ear implies sound, the existence of the conscience implies God. The existence of conscience implies the existence of a moral code that strongly suggests the reality of an external absolute. And, as we explained in chapter 4, no absolute for morality will suffice except God.

The bleakness of unbelievers' view of the universe may lead them to deny that thinking can lead to any true conclusions. But they still must believe the conclusions of their own thinking. They can't help it. When they claim there are no absolutes, they must believe that this claim, at least, is absolute. At the very least they must believe their thinking is true when it leads them to conclude that there can be no truth. And they must find some way to live with the convoluted inconsistency of such a conclusion. The very nature of the universe forces unbelievers to live and think in ways that are inconsistent with their unbelief. They must isolate themselves from the rational nature of the universe and lock themselves inside a cell of irrationality. But the rational universe continually seeps in from every crack and corner, challenging their illusions with strong doses of reality. Believing that conscience, reason, morality, self, and truth are not there does not make unbelievers immune to their effects. Unbelievers are like young Neal in the following limerick:

'Twas said by a young man named Neal,
  Who insisted that pain was not real,
    "When I sit on a pin,
    And it punctures my skin,
  I dislike what I fancy I feel."

Many today like to think that whatever they choose to believe becomes real for them. But reality grants no exemptions. Thinking the stove is not hot will not keep it from burning a man who puts his hand to it.

THE RELENTLESSNESS OF REALITY

Unbelievers unwittingly depend on God as the basis for their argument against God. Their complaint that the universe is meaningless is a tacit admission that meaning must exist. The fact that human beings have a concept of meaning is telling. It demonstrates that, whether or not we believe meaning actually exists, we can at least imagine its existence. And it is impossible to imagine anything that is completely outside our own experience. The most creative human thinkers merely discover, reorder, and synthesize elements collected from their senses and experiences. They never come up with anything truly new.

For example, try to imagine a new primary color, a sixth sense, a fourth dimension, or a third sex that is not a combination or extension of those that exist already. Of course we can claim to imagine things we have neither seen nor experienced—flying cows, strangely shaped alien beings, or water running uphill. But such mental fabrications are assembled from the raw material we have gathered from actual experience. Even the incredibly creative Albert Einstein, who postulated a fourth dimension that included time and curved space, had the raw materials of time and solid geometry to work with. As a successful book publisher once said, "If you steal from one source, it's called plagiarism. If you steal from two or more sources, it's called creativity." Beneath his humor was a solid point. Recombining or reshaping what we have experienced through our senses is the limit of what we can create or even imagine.

The fact that we can imagine, comprehend, or even deny the concept of meaning shows that meaning does exist. Otherwise, we could never have thought of it. It is impossible to complain of meaninglessness unless we have some idea of what meaning should be, which proves that meaning is a reality that has somehow managed to invade our experience. If light had never existed, it would be impossible for us to imagine it and we would not know to complain of darkness. In a world where all was truly meaningless, the idea of meaning would never occur to us, and we would be incapable of complaining of its absence. The idea of meaning is with us because meaning is a reality of the universe we live in, and we cannot escape the innate sense of purpose that emanates like an aroma from every created thing.

This sense of meaning points directly to an absolute, and the only absolute that can provide meaning is the God who created this universe for a specific purpose. We find meaning for our own lives when we discover how our individual purpose fits into his purpose. There is no escape. The absolute from outside the natural universe continually invades every corner of unbelievers' lives and thinking. Even when they step off the cliff of irrationality, God is the unyielding truth that meets them at the bottom.

THE UNTENABLE POSITION OF ATHEISM

Atheism is so thoroughly at odds with reality that it does not spring forth naturally or deeply rooted from the depths of the heart. It is always based on delusion. Atheists, like everyone else, begin life with an intuitive but dormant sense of the reality of God ready to be cultivated into full belief. Unless sidetracked by training, anger, pride, resentment, or immorality, people will bend naturally toward belief.

If we could peel away all the layers of atheists' denial, we would find that they are potential believers who have chosen not to activate their innate capacity for belief. They have chosen to cling to something that is mutually exclusive to belief in God, so they buried their God awareness in order to get on with their wants. Perhaps many of them, like poet William Ernest Henley, simply want a universe wherein they can say, "I am the master of my fate: I am the captain of my soul."[3] They do not want to place themselves under the authority of a higher power that may have claims on them, so they deny that any higher power exists in order to maintain the illusion of self-mastery. Theirs is not a solid, insoluble conviction. And if either atheism or belief in God must be wrong (as one or the other must), it is the atheists who are in greater jeopardy.

Some atheists must shout their denial of God shrilly and continually to keep the relentless awareness of God buried. But someday it will certainly emerge because no lie can survive for long in a universe built on the absolute of truth. A lie has no real existence. Anything that is not true is merely the noise of a moment, a dying echo that reveals its hollowness against the unmoving walls of reality.

Atheists' avoidance of God is based on a misunderstanding of what God means to mankind. Many atheists want independence from God in order to claim freedom for themselves. English novelist Aldous Huxley said, "I had motives for not wanting the world to have meaning, consequently assumed it had none. . . . For myself, as no doubt for most of my contemporaries, the philosophy of meaninglessness was essentially an instrument of liberation. The liberation we desired was simultaneously liberation from a certain political and economic system and liberation from a certain system of morality. We objected to the morality because it interfered with our sexual freedom."[4] Those who turn to atheism to escape from God do not realize that a relationship with him promises more freedom than they can ever find on their own terms. Atheists running from God are like captive animals running from the zookeeper who has entered the cage to free them. Atheists will remain imprisoned within themselves and their constricted universe until they allow God to lead them to freedom.

The simple fact of God's existence is enough to give anyone a strong sense of meaning. Meaning is what drew my agnostic friend to Christianity. Even if there were no promise of life after death, just knowing that God exists bathes the universe with purpose and glory that vanishes when we see it as the product of blind chance. Yet the wonder of it all is that when we turn to God, we gain this assurance of meaning not only in a theoretical sense but also in a direct and personal sense. The God of the universe wants a personal relationship with us and offers to share eternity with us. We are designed for relationship, and this invitation to a relationship with God is our ultimate source of meaning.

When you get right down to it, believing in God is the only rational option. While there is no way to prove his existence empirically, we must believe in him to make any sense out of existence itself. Nothing fits together as it should or has any real meaning unless God is the absolute behind it all. The universe takes on meaning only because God made it and has a plan for it. And your life takes on meaning because he created you for a particular purpose, which you can find when you come into a proper relationship with him.

QUESTIONS FOR THOUGHT AND DISCUSSION

1. In a naturalistic universe, why are humans no more meaningful than bugs, weeds, rocks, or any other natural phenomena?
2. If human beings are accidental machines, can we rationally judge any person's actions to be good or evil? Why or why not?
3. Why is there no possible source of meaning in a completely naturalistic universe?
4. Why is the position of not believing in God at odds with reality?
5. Why do believers and unbelievers alike tend to justify their wrong behavior?
6. What have many atheists done with their innate God-consciousness? Why?
7. What is the only ultimate source of meaning in the universe? Why?

CHAPTER SIX

WHY DO WE LOVE SUNSETS AND SYMPHONIES?

Y ou attend a symphony concert, and the orchestra performs a
concerto that lifts your soul and sets it soaring. The music
moves you so deeply that it literally makes the hair on your neck
stand on end. You wonder how music can evoke such powerful
emotions.

You visit a gallery and stand before a painting of such stunning
color, depth, and substance that it takes your breath away and
makes your heart beat faster.

You round the bend on a rugged mountain trail and stop dead
in your tracks in awe of the vista before you. A glorious snow-
capped peak gleams in the sun, its grandeur reflected in a pristine
lake rimmed with towering pines. You are overcome with longings
and aspirations you can neither identify nor explain.

You gaze in rapt fascination as an Olympic skater glides, leaps,
and spins with uncanny grace and balance. As the performance

ends, you and hundreds of others spontaneously rise to your feet to cheer and applaud.

On some enchanted evening, across a crowded room you see a face that captivates you completely. You know you will never be content gazing at anyone else.

In each of these settings you are experiencing the mystery of beauty—immersing yourself in the deep, inner pleasure we receive in response to certain combinations of forms, colors, textures, sounds, or movements. For the purposes of our discussion, beauty includes all objects, sights, sounds, or experiences that stir us to awe, elation, inspiration, enchantment, delight, or ecstasy. Beauty is what lifts life above the mundane and prosaic and gives it joy.

We are hard-pressed to explain why encounters with beauty affect us so profoundly. What is there about a song, a snow-capped mountain, a work of art, or a certain face that so grips our hearts and thrills our souls? Despite the high place we give beauty in our lives, our attempts to define it fall short.

EXPLANATIONS FOR BEAUTY

For the most part we don't even try to define beauty but simply explain it away as something altogether subjective. When people express differing aesthetic preferences, the usual response is that "beauty is in the eye of the beholder." I like the mountains; you prefer the seashore. I enjoy classical music; you're into country. I appreciate the French Impressionists; you prefer Andy Warhol. I like colonial architecture; you like the glass and steel lines of city skyscrapers. Because of such broadly differing preferences, most of us feel that standards for beauty are not objective but determined solely by personal taste. Even believers tend to think that, unlike the absolute of morality, beauty is a matter of individual preference.

However, our variations in preferences are minor compared to the vast sea of common agreement we share about what is beautiful and what is not. For example, almost everyone considers swans and butterflies beautiful but bats and spiders ugly. Most of us see beauty in an Alpine vista of snow-capped mountains, but few see it in an ash-coated landscape devastated by a volcanic eruption. While men differ over whether they favor blondes, brunettes, or redheads, all agree that some particular women are beautiful regardless of their hair color. While the eyes of individual beholders may have preferences, these preferences are only variations within great, common themes of beauty that virtually all people recognize.

Naturalists tend to explain beauty in terms of pragmatic function. What we call beauty in living creatures, they see as features that evolved to protect and propagate the various species. To them the brilliant color of a flower has nothing to do with our joy and delight in it; it is merely nature's signal to attract butterflies and bees for the purpose of cross-pollination. Naturalists would say that the feminine physical features we call beautiful were not designed for their aesthetic effect; they attract men because they display a woman's capacity to bear and nurture children. A man's broad shoulders and bulging biceps attract females simply because they display his ability to protect and provide. A peacock spreads its gorgeous plumage to attract a peahen. The splendid stripes of a tiger merely camouflage the animal as it stalks its prey in tall grass. To naturalists, what we call beauty is no mystery at all. It is the by-product of nature's practical means for propagating and preserving life on the planet.

In art and design, naturalists give beauty a similar explanation. They say that what we call beauty is simply that which displays efficiency and functionality. Architect Frank Lloyd Wright's famous maxim "form follows function" summarized his belief that designing for efficiency tends to result in beauty. The supersonic Concorde aircraft has been called the most beautiful machine in the world. Someone once asked its designer how much effort he put into giving the plane its extraordinary elegance and grace. He replied that he gave no thought whatever to making the plane beautiful. Every contour was plotted solely to make the plane fly as efficiently as possible. His success at utility gave the plane beauty as a natural by-product.

It is tempting to think that efficiency and functionality may be the keys to the mystery of beauty. Things that function efficiently do tend to be what we call beautiful, whereas things that are clumsy or defective do not. Health is beautiful while sickness and decay are not. Life is beautiful, and death is a horror. Harmony is beautiful, and dissonance is repelling. Order is beautiful, whereas chaos and imbalance make us uneasy and tense. Beauty seems to grow out of efficiency. We don't find beauty in waste, decay, brokenness, or malfunction.

This explanation holds much truth, but it has too many exceptions to be the whole story. Efficient function often exists independently of beauty. Two people may be equally strong, healthy, hardworking, and efficient, but one may have beauty while the other is homely. Despite architect Wright's theory, the popularity of restoring Victorian and antebellum houses tells us that many people find beauty in ornamentation that has no practical function at all. If efficiency and functionality are beautiful, why does almost everyone find even harmless spiders hideous? Music has no apparent utilitarian function at all, yet its pleasure is so lavish and spectacular that our response to it is often nothing short of ecstatic. If death is a horror, why is no season of the year more beautiful than autumn, which owes its spectacular color to dying tree leaves? And if life itself is intrinsically beautiful, how do we explain our extreme revulsion at a colony of teeming maggots?

Some philosophers have explained beauty in terms of harmony, symmetry, proportion, rhythm, and archetypes. Any or all of these qualities may be helpful in analyzing what factors in nature or art trigger rapturous responses in us, but none explains why we experience such rapture when our senses encounter them. An airtight explanation for beauty eludes us. Why we get such pleasure in seeing certain forms, hearing certain sounds, and feeling certain textures remains a baffling question. But our purpose here is not to answer that question. It is to show that while we cannot understand or define beauty, it is not an illusion. It is not solely utilitarian, and it is not totally subjective. Beauty exists as an objective reality, and nothing within nature will account for it. Beauty points us toward a certainty that an absolute exists somewhere above nature.

TURNING REALITY WRONG SIDE OUT

Naturalistic explanations for beauty don't work because they turn reality wrong side out. Naturalism reduces everything in nature to a mechanical function. But reality presents itself to us the other way around. Naturalists see the mechanics that keep nature running as the sum total of reality, whereas believers see the mechanics as only the means to achieve the purpose of why things exist. The mechanics are merely the innards, while all the meaning is found in the function that the mechanics produce. The naturalists' philosophy is wrong side out because it mistakes the mechanics for the meaning.

To illustrate, consider your computer. The electrical impulses, printed circuits, drives, disks, and chips inside your computer are what make your computer work, but they are not the meaning and purpose of your computer. What gives your computer meaning and purpose is how it helps you work, learn, and communicate. The mechanics are important not for their own sakes but only because they give you what you see on your screen and print on your printer. The meaning of a clock is not in its springs and gears but in its face, where it reports the time. The mechanics are the means of producing meaning, not meaning itself.

The naturalists' universe is wrong side out because they insist that there is nothing more to it than the machinery that keeps it running. The blind, purposeless functioning of all nature is to them the sum total of reality. Naturalists do not admit to meaning and purpose in the universe because such an admission implies that meaning and purpose came first and that the mechanics were designed to achieve them. This implication requires a designer, something the naturalistic worldview cannot allow. To naturalists, accidental, meaningless mechanics must be the sum total of reality.

The world of the naturalist has no place for beauty. In seeing the universe solely as a mechanism, they lose all that gives it beauty because they can see no truth deeper than what they find in the analysis of its parts. They find no meaning or purpose behind the analysis, and the result is a loss of mystery and art. Dogged naturalists cannot admit the grandeur of a snow-capped mountain because grandeur is a concept that requires more meaning than mere mechanics can provide. All they can allow themselves to see in the mountain are solidified minerals of the earth's crust broken and thrust upward by random geologic forces. They cannot allow any sense of art or meaning to the arrangement of the forms, textures, light, and color of the peak. They cannot allow themselves to feel any sense of awe or delight in the extravagant forms of nature.

They close their ears to any invitation to lay aside their analytic X-ray lens and join the dance.

To sit down to a breakfast of bacon, eggs, honey, and milk is a great pleasure for most of us. But if all we can see on that plate are fatty slivers from the stomach of a mud-wallowing mammal, the ovulation of a large fowl coagulated by heat, sticky secretions from the reproductive organs of plants mixed with the saliva of an insect, and the discharge from the mammary gland of a ruminating mammal, we are likely to lose our appetites. Yet this is the breakfast naturalists sit down to every morning. This outlook that reduces to mechanics all that gives delight to the senses reflects their philosophy of all nature. When they look out their window at what believers see as trees, shrubs, flowers, and grass, naturalists see masses of roots, follicles, fibers, and pulps with tentacles clutching the earth, sucking nutrients from it like parasitic lampreys. When naturalists look at a spring leaf, they do not see the glory of existence in its form, color, and texture. Instead they see only the chemicals and mechanics of sap, photons, veins, and tissues. The green of the leaf does not inspire them to wonder and delight; it is merely the mechanical result of photosynthesis turning light rays into chlorophyll and has no more claim to beauty than the green excretion of an infected bile duct.

THE NATURALISTIC INCONSISTENCY

You may think it's pretty presumptuous of us to portray the way all naturalists look at nature. And in a way, it is. What we have been describing is the way unbelievers *should* see nature if they remain consistent with their philosophy. But the fact is, in spite of holding to a philosophy that logically excludes beauty, most unbelievers do respond to beauty much as believers do. They can hardly help it. Intellectually, they may say that a gloriously colorful and fragrant orchid is merely a function of a mechanistic universe, but when they gaze at such a flower, it has the same emotional impact on most of them as it does on believers. Naturalists may explain the spectrum of color inherent in the sun's light in strictly scientific terms, but they are as likely as believers to feel awe and wonder at a sunset.

Here is the reason: Beauty is a reality so much stronger than naturalistic philosophy that it simply storms past their intellect and acts directly on their emotions. It's likely that most naturalists have not thought through their position to its logical conclusion. They don't realize that they cannot remain consistent naturalists and yet believe in beauty. But for those unfortunate enough to have a strong commitment to both consistency and naturalistic philosophy, the light of beauty can no longer shine.

If you think we are overstating the case, listen to the pitiable lament of scientist and poet George John Romanes, a believer in creation until he abandoned his faith to become a disciple of Darwin. "I am not ashamed to confess that with this virtual negation of God the universe to me has lost its soul of loveliness; . . . when at times I think, as think at times I must, of the appalling contrast between the hallowed glory of that creed which once was mine, and the lonely mystery of existence as I now find it—at such times I shall ever feel it impossible to avoid the sharpest pang of which my nature is susceptible."[1]

Romanes expressed the tragic despair of all thinking people who allow their philosophy to distort their view of reality to the point that they reject the absolute who gives meaning and beauty to existence.

When Romanes turned to naturalism, he turned the universe wrong side out. The innards came to the surface, and all he could see was the viscera of reality—the mechanical workings, the chugging, pulsating engine of nature fueling itself on itself, producing nothing important, designed for no purpose, but running on aimlessly like a Rube Goldberg machine until it finally peters out. When Romanes excluded God from his world, all that could give meaning to its forms, textures, colors, and sounds evaporated. He was left in a lonely, darkened world haunted by an illusion of beauty that his new philosophy forced him to reject.

Naturalists may regard beauty as an illusion, but it is an illusion they cannot ignore. It is perhaps the only thing in their mechanistic universe that can divert their minds from the tragic reality of the ultimate oblivion of all things, including themselves. It is better to dance on the edge of the gaping grave than to sit brooding over its inevitability.

The direction that much art has taken in the past few generations tells us something about the despair of naturalism. There was a time when the goal of the artist was to display beauty. But as naturalistic philosophy became dominant, much of the art produced became increasingly pointless, despairing, and consciously devoid of beauty. The oppressive weight of the philosophy of meaninglessness has squeezed the bright colors from the brushes of many unbelieving artists. In their despair they have dismissed beauty as an illusion that cannot hide the dark void they believe will ultimately engulf all things. And their art reflects that despair.

We have asserted that in a truly naturalistic world, beauty cannot logically exist. Here is why. Beauty implies an ideal. The concept of beauty suggests standards that an object must meet or approach to achieve perfection. The more nearly an object comes to matching the ideal for its kind, the more beautiful it is. But in a naturalistic, accidental world with no absolutes no such ideals or standards are possible. What is merely is; there is no such thing as what ought to be. We must have a standard that defines what ought to be before we can evaluate whether a form meets that standard. But in a world without God, all forms and functions are accidental and, according to evolution, in a state of perpetual change, drifting on the currents of natural selection, punctuated equilibrium, mutation, and endless adaptation. We cannot freeze the evolutionary frame and claim that at any given moment a given form is ideal. In a world of such fluctuation, we can have no fixed, absolute standards to which we can expect anything to conform. We can have no beauty without such standards, no standards without absolutes, and no absolutes in an accidental, mechanical world without God. If the naturalists are right, true beauty cannot exist, for you cannot find a fixed, unchanging standard to which beauty should measure up.

THE BELIEVER'S EXPLANATION

How do believers explain the ecstatic human response to a Schubert symphony or a Raphael painting, the stunning power of a west Texas sunset, or the feelings of sublimity evoked by a mountain waterfall? Naturalists assert that such feelings are only subjective, that nothing in the waterfall itself is inherently sublime. It only seems sublime because it arouses feelings of awe in the viewer.

Refuting such a view, C. S. Lewis, in his book *The Abolition of Man,* asserts that certain emotional responses are appropriate to certain objects in nature. Unless the waterfall has some inherent quality that elicits the awe the viewer senses, such feelings are absurd and inexplicable.

What quality can a waterfall, a sunset, or a mountain have that makes feelings of awe appropriate? Naturalists will say that the mountain's craggy surface thrusting upward toward the clouds is merely the result of tectonic mechanics—the random geologic forces beneath the crust of the earth. A waterfall is nothing more than gravity's inevitable effect on flowing liquid at the point where the river channel ends at a precipice. But how do they explain the lofty feelings these natural geologic phenomena evoke? Such feelings make no sense in a totally naturalistic universe. Something more is involved here than gravity and geology.

The mountain may be a work of art. That is, a creator may have purposefully willed its form to evoke in us a specific effect. We may not know exactly what effect this creator intended, but we can extrapolate a possibility from feelings common to so many people that they may be considered universal. To most viewers, mountains evoke feelings of sublimity, of upward aspiration, of majesty, of awe, of mystical reaching toward the heavens. Perhaps the mountain was created to be a visual metaphor for our longing to touch something above and beyond our experience. Like Plato's "shadows in a cave," mountains, sunsets, and beautiful music and art may be dim hints of greater realities that exist in a supernatural realm above our own. The beauty we experience in nature and express in art may be echoes from beyond nature telling us that something more than what we see here exists, and what we see here is merely a lesser image of it.

It is those dreamers among us, those incurable romantics who come closest to the truth about creation. It is in those moments when we feel the grandeur of the mountain, when the landscape is breathtaking, when the tree leaves glow with magical light, when the music seems to tingle with the essence of life, when the face at which we gaze seems to glow with the magical light of a goddess that the veil is lifted and we see reality for what it is. The naturalists' analytic lens that dismisses such experiences as nothing more than mechanics and chemicals misses reality by a tree-lined, brook-rippling, bird-chirping country mile.

Yes, we know all about the other side of nature—death, decay, pain, heartache, cancers, grief, heart attacks, hurricanes, floods, tornadoes, and earthquakes. These woes are terrible, but they are only temporary blights on reality, not reality itself. For several years my route to work took me across a metal bridge spanning the Colorado River near Austin, Texas. Every inch of that bridge's surface is covered with rust. Even though I could not actually see the substance of the bridge because of its rust coating, I would never assert that the rust is the reality of the bridge. The truth about the bridge is the solid metal beneath the rust. The truth about creation is the glory beneath the blight that mars it. The romantics so ridiculed in today's world are really the ones with the clearest eyes. They see through the fog that clouds the vision of the rest of us. And in seeing beauty for what it is, they see the truth.

Yet, for all the longings beauty arouses in us, nothing in nature or art will fully answer them. No melody, however skillfully adorned with harmonies or sensitively performed, satisfies the unnamed desires it arouses in our souls. No man or woman, however perfect in face and form, however delightful in personality, however lovely in spirit, however loving and devoted, quite fills the yearning of one heart to merge with another. Despite the longing we feel as we stand before a majestic peak, there is nothing about the mountain itself that we desire. The inherent quality of the mountain that causes the longing is merely a shadow of something greater. The mountain is not the object we desire, but it does point us toward it.

These objects of beauty are only shadows, though lovely ones, of a reality we desire, a reality that is yet unseen, unheard, and un-felt. The beauty in nature stirs up a "memory" of something we were meant to enjoy but have never fully experienced. It's as if something hovers at the edge of our comprehension that requires a sense not yet developed in order to grasp it fully. Yet we can occasionally catch dim, fleeting glimpses of it through the five senses we do have.

Beauty calls with a siren's voice, and our longing to abandon all and chase after it is almost overwhelming. But we find that beauty is like the rainbow's end: It beckons but eludes. It's a shimmering soap bubble that disappears in our grasping hand. In the presence of beauty we are like a child with her nose pressed to the window of a toy store. We look and yearn, but we find a barrier that prevents the full experience of what is before us. As much as we long to immerse ourselves in the beauty we see, we can't do it. Even at the most intense moment of ecstasy in our experience of the symphony, the sunset, the painting, or the embrace, we realize that what we really long for is yet beyond. These wonderful things are only images of the real object of our desire, and that object remains as elusive as ever. Whatever it is that we long for, beauty is not it. Beauty is merely the doorway to it.

In beauty we hear the chords of the supernatural reverberating within nature. Beauty invites us to see within nature and art that greater reality in which everything has its origin. Beauty in its full-ness remains elusive to us because it emanates from a dimension that is closed off to us. We live within nature—a nature so fallen that it taints all the beauty that shines on it from the dimension of the supernatural. Yet beauty breaks through the cloud of the Fall and bathes all nature with a glory that declares the transcendent source of all things. The glimpses of beauty that invade our world are tangible evidence that beauty in its fullness does exist. And that taste of beauty underscores the promise that we can ultimately ascend to that dimension and find the true object of our desire. But not yet. For now our place is in our own world, where we have tasks to be done and duties to be performed before we can abandon all and pursue the beauty that so tantalizes us. We can't taste the wine until we have trod out the grapes.

Many poets, composers, and writers have eloquently expressed this overpowering yearning to abandon all and plunge headlong after beauty. *The Lord of the Rings* author J. R. R. Tolkien, in his short story "Leaf by Niggle," tells of a struggling artist so enamored with the beauty of leaves that he devotes his life to painting them. But in time the artist discovers that there is a greater beauty than the leaf and begins to paint the entire tree, then the forest, then the vista beyond the forest, then the light that gives glory to the vista. Niggle would devote every waking moment to the pursuit of his unfolding vision of beauty, but the recurring needs of his sickly neighbor frequently interrupt him and prevent him from ever finishing his painting.

Sir Arthur Sullivan, the composer half of the Gilbert and Sullivan team, in his stirring song "The Lost Chord" portrays a weary composer sitting at an organ keyboard. As his fingers roam absently across the keys, he unwittingly strikes an incredibly beautiful chord of music "like the sound of the great Amen." The unearthly majesty of the chord moves him to the core as it "leapt from the soul of the organ and entered into mine." He anxiously tries to form the chord again, but to no avail. He finally realizes that the chord was not native to this earth, and though the echoes of it will linger in his heart for the rest of his days, only in heaven will he actually hear it again.

In his poem "Stopping by Woods on a Snowy Evening," Robert Frost tells of passing a lovely, quiet woods during a beautiful snowfall. The poet pauses as a compelling desire draws him to enter the woods and immerse himself in its idyllic serenity, to become one with it and find rest there. But he cannot. He knows that the peace and loveliness that draw him toward the woods are not yet his to claim. He and the beauty he sees are of different worlds. His is the world of duty to others like himself, people who must struggle against adversity, pain, loss, grief, and want. He must maintain his loyalty to others in the fallen world before he can enter the perfect one. He must maintain his focus and complete his course. He sadly prods his horse forward, sighing as he passes,

> The woods are lovely, dark and deep,
> But I have promises to keep,
> And miles to go before I sleep,
> And miles to go before I sleep.

THE IMAGE OF PERFECTION

Christian theology provides the reason for our desire for and alienation from beauty. It tells us that we are fallen creatures living in a fallen world. Originally, all creation emanated perfect, unsullied beauty, but it incurred damage, and the beauty became blighted. Now all beauty is, at best, flawed. No form is quite symmetrical, no face is without blemish, no color pure, no balance perfect, no harmony without a touch of dissonance. A veil has been drawn between our world and the source of all perfect beauty.

A shadowy but tantalizing image of this perfect beauty that exists beyond the veil remains locked away in every human heart. This is why those dim rays of beauty that filter into our flawed world so arrest our attention and touch our emotions. At such moments we sense the existence of that original perfection that is now beyond our capacity to experience fully. A vision of what was meant to be flashes across the screen of our consciousness like a subliminal image, and we are hooked. We long for the full experience of what we can now only glimpse.

We can only glimpse because beauty in its unfallen fullness is presently beyond the capacity of our fallen senses. But the flawed beauty that lingers in our world assures us of the greater reality that exists beyond the horizon. And this awareness that beauty is real but presently unattainable is the source of both our longing and our alienation.

Beauty is a strong indication that ideals are real. The more nearly a form, sound, or color approximates its unseen ideal, the more beautiful it is. And ideals imply absolutes. To borrow an illustration from Plato, if the flawed beauty we see in nature is a shadow, a reality must exist outside nature to form the shadow and a light must exist behind the reality to cast it. And realities are always greater than their shadows. For beauty to exist, there must be a God who designed it as the ultimate expression of perfection. All beauty is an invitation to look beyond nature and art to embrace the greater reality that is the invisible object of our desire. The beauty of a magnificent painting calls us to engage the artist. The spine-tingling harmonies of a grand anthem point us in the direction of the composer. A mountain sunrise, a delicate flower, the power and skill of an Olympic athlete, the grace of a soaring eagle draw us toward their designer.

Beauty not only points us toward God but also reveals something of God's nature that even believers often find surprising. Just as reason shows the consistency of God and morality shows the character of God, beauty shows, if we can open our minds to see it, the emotion of God. Beauty is the joy, the delight, the smile, and the laughter of God—the ecstasy of God. Beauty reveals that God desires not that we merely exist but that we revel in supreme delight. Beauty shows that the world is infused with more meaning than mere mechanics can account for—meaning to be experienced in joy and ecstasy. We have hints and echoes and vibrations of it throughout all creation. And these daily promises of ultimate beauty make life precious and worthwhile, even within the pains and disasters of this fallen world.

This truth about beauty highlights the tragedy of the naturalists. Their world of mechanistic and aimless function is a poor substitute for the hints of sublime reality that beauty promises. Puddleglum, the marshwiggle in C. S. Lewis's children's book *The Silver Chair,* stated it powerfully. Trapped by an evil queen in an underground world of dark caves, dim lights, hellish fires, and putrid swamps far beneath the bright, fair land of Narnia, Puddleglum is drugged and enchanted into almost believing that he has made up the idea of the beautiful Narnia with its golden lion, Aslan. The queen tells him that the dreary, black caverns that imprison him are all that exist. But in a speech both heroic and eloquent, Puddleglum shakes off the illusion and tells the queen,

> Suppose we *have* only dreamed, or made up, all those things—trees and grass and sun and moon and stars and Aslan himself. Suppose we have. Then all I can say is that, in that case, the made-up things seem a good deal more important than the real ones. Suppose this black pit of a kingdom of yours *is* the only world. Well, it strikes me as

a pretty poor one. . . . That's why I'm going to stand by the play-world. I'm on Aslan's side even if there isn't any Aslan to lead it. I'm going to live as like a Narnian as I can even if there isn't any Narnia.[2]

When naturalists shut out God, they banish themselves to an underground world devoid of drama, wonder, glory, and mystery. It is a poor substitute for the beauty-saturated world of believers.

Naturalism is inadequate to account for beauty. Beauty growing out of naturalism is like a rose growing out of a dunghill. If the dunghill is all that exists, we have no way to account for the rose. But, of course, the rose is easy to explain if we assume the dunghill is not all that exists—that a seed was dropped into it from a source above it. And this is exactly the position of believers. Unbelievers should at least take a hard look at the possibility that beauty is no illusion. Beauty leads us to certainty that just outside our field of vision is a living power who cares for us and wants us to experience delight.

But we must beware. Beauty exerts such a pull on our souls that many turn to it as the ultimate experience, trying to find fulfillment in what is only a pointer to a greater reality. We all have heard others say they find their greatest spiritual experiences in nature or art or music or their loved one. God's greatest gifts can most easily become substitutes for God himself.

Beauty apart from its source is not enough to give us lasting joy; it is merely a guide to joy and an enhancement of it. God gave us beauty to lead us to him. It is in relationship to him that we experience the essence of beauty.

QUESTIONS FOR THOUGHT AND DISCUSSION

1. Does beauty exist only in the eye of the beholder? Why or why not?
2. How do naturalists define beauty?
3. How does the naturalistic view of beauty turn reality "wrong side out"?
4. Why do naturalists resist the idea that beauty suggests meaning and purpose?
5. How do believers define beauty?
6. In what ways does beauty point to the supernatural?
7. Why is beauty unable to satisfy the longings it arouses? What will satisfy those longings?
8. Why is it impossible to find spiritual fulfillment in getting alone with nature?

CHAPTER SEVEN

IS THE UNIVERSE A COSMIC ACCIDENT?

THE IRRATIONALITY OF EVOLUTION

Most of us have spent summer nights lying on the lawn, gazing into the sparkling mystery of deep heaven. We locate the North Star, the Big Dipper, the gossamer haze of the Milky Way, and other easily identified constellations and planets against a backdrop of countless celestial bodies. As we stare in awe, it dawns on us that all the stars we see are within our own galaxy, which is one galaxy among billions that fill deep space. We begin to feel small as we realize that our home planet is only a speck in a vast universe that extends in all directions without end.

At about this point the gears in our brain begin to grind as we grapple with concepts beyond our capacity even to imagine. Surely nothing can stretch on and on without ultimately ending somewhere. Yet when we try to imagine a limit to the universe—maybe an enormous wall or some astronomically gigantic glass bubble—we then face the question, what's outside this bubble? We find it impossible to imagine space with limits or without limits. The impossible but inevitable concept of infinite space is simply more than our minds can handle.

Thinking about time presents the same dilemma. We can't conceive of a beginning or an ending of time because the only thing we can imagine beyond it is just more time. Since everything we experience has a beginning and an ending, the concept of eternity is incomprehensible to us.

We have the same problem with matter—the stuff the universe is made of. Has matter always existed, or did everything come into being from nothing at some point in the past? Either option is unfathomable to our finite minds. The well-known big bang theory, which postulates that our universe is the result of a cataclysmic explosion, does not answer the question. The theory assumes the existence of a small, incredibly dense mass of condensed matter before the bang. How did this ball of matter come to exist?

The most controversial of these questions is, how did life begin? Was it a blind accident or a deliberate act? Or has life always existed without a beginning? These questions were not much of an issue until Charles Darwin introduced his watershed theory for the origin of life. Since then creation and evolution have been hotly debated with neither side willing to concede an inch.

In the search for certainty, we must grapple with the issue of origins, especially the origin of life. Can we find bedrock for our belief in a creator? Or do the naturalists have just as much foundation for their view of origins? In order to answer these questions, we begin by taking on the issue of evolution.

WHAT'S WRONG WITH EVOLUTION?

In the secular world, the most widely accepted explanation for the origin of life grew out of the Darwinian theory called the evolution of the species.[1] The theory of evolution has a number of variations and is in a continual state of flux, but in general it claims that life began accidentally. According to the theory, a delicately balanced combination of chemicals happened to fuse together under ideal conditions to form a simple organic cell. An electrical current jolted the cell to life, and it began to reproduce itself through mitosis.

In time these reproducing cells combined with others in increasingly complex patterns to form simple plants and animals. The theory posits that over millions of years of change, some of the animals acquired and developed a measure of intelligence. After many stages of evolution spanning millions of years, one branch of the intelligent animal kingdom became human.

Most of us lack the scientific knowledge to understand the complex arguments formulated to support evolution. But all of these arguments tend to divert us from the main point. The proof of evolution is not to be found in the study of natural selection, mutations, or the dating or interpreting of fossils. These and other supports for the theory are only the foliage of a theory that is fatally diseased at the root. You don't need a Ph.D. in paleontology or biology to see through the foliage and find the moribund trunk of evolution. Common, everyday reason exposes this theory as a fantasy.

Evolution calls for the suspension of natural laws that have never been observed to have exceptions. The case for evolution rests on assumptions that three things have happened, each of which demands an exception to the natural order of the universe. No one has ever observed these occurrences in action; science cannot cause them to happen; and reason says they cannot happen. Yet the theory of evolution can be true only if they did happen. We will briefly consider these assumptions one by one then spend the rest of the chapter exploring their implications.

1. Evolution assumes that order can emerge naturally out of chaos.
This assumption runs counter to a firmly established, inviolable
natural law. Chaos never produces order. Yet for evolution to
make sense, we must believe that aimless, undirected atoms and
molecules could pull themselves together and arrange themselves
into increasingly more complex and orderly forms. That's like believing that leaky buckets dripping in a paint factory could produce the Mona Lisa. No law of nature can account for order
coming out of chaos, and the idea contradicts inviolable laws of entropy, which say, in a nutshell, that everything is running down.
Left to itself, nature scatters, erodes, breaks down, and wears out.
Life always plays out into death; the organic decays into the inorganic. Stars burn out and disintegrate. Planets slow infinitesimally
with each orbit. Energy is consumed, and resources are depleted,
never to be fully replaced in the cycle of nature. We consistently
observe a universe that is irrevocably running down.

But evolution asks us to believe that exceptions to the laws of
entropy have occurred, that in pockets of the universe things are
becoming increasingly more orderly, organized, and efficient. Unfortunately for the theory, no evidence of such upward progress
exists, and no known scientific principle can account for it.

2. Evolution assumes that all life emerged from dead matter. Life
emerging from lifeless matter violates both reason and solid scientific principles. Death simply cannot produce life. Never in the history of our world has anyone caused life to start up from dead
matter or witnessed such a phenomenon. Nor has the theory been
proven by scientific experiment, though many have been tried.
Theorists have outlined in detail the conditions of the elements
and the sequence of events that caused that first cell to be spontaneously shocked to life. But no one has ever been able to create a

single organic cell or bring a dead cell to life even under the most carefully controlled laboratory conditions. Science, experience, and common sense show us plainly and without exception that life comes only from pre-existing life. A totally naturalistic universe that begins with nothing in it but dead, inorganic elements will remain dead and inorganic. To believe otherwise is to turn a rational, foundational principle of science upside down.

3. *Evolution assumes that human intelligence and reason evolved from dead matter.* According to the theory, no thinking, reasoning organisms existed when the big bang went off. But out of that mindless chaos eventually came the ultra complex computer called the human brain with its ability to reason.

What natural force could have brought such a thing into being? What principle operating in nature accounts for the spontaneous appearance of a self-aware, thinking organism arising out of formless gases and inanimate minerals? The answer is simple: There is no such force or principle.

These three foundation blocks of evolution are flawed by the same basic irrationality. They ask us to believe that something can be generated from nothing, that things can give more than they have, that the engine can start on an empty tank and with no hand to turn the key. We learned in high school science classes that such things simply do not and cannot happen. Both science and reason agree (as true science and true reason always do) that no effect can be greater than its cause. A baseball that leaves the pitcher's hand at 80 mph will not pick up speed and cross the plate at 90 mph. A rubber ball will not bounce higher than the point from which you drop it. You can't feed a hen one pound of grain and expect her to lay two pounds of eggs. Nothing can give more than it has. A universe that begins in lifeless chaos will remain lifeless and chaotic.

This rigid law of cause and effect governs all the activity in the universe. Yet evolution asks us to suspend reason and assume an exception has occurred despite the fact that no exception has ever been observed or demonstrated.

IS EVOLUTION SCIENCE OR THEORY?

Lurking behind evolution is the philosophy of an irrational universe. As we concluded in chapter 3, this is the only kind of universe you can have when you remove God from it, and the theory of evolution demonstrates the truth of this conclusion. Pure science that simply observes, experiments, and reports shows us an orderly universe of unalterable law and reason. Evolution demands that we deny what we see and allow the possibility of irrational exceptions to the rational laws of cause and effect. Evolutionists know they can't have it both ways: They can't have the universe as it is defined by science and simultaneously embrace a theory that contradicts science. To resolve the dilemma, they have pounded the round peg of irrational evolution into the square hole of rational science, ignoring the splinters and claiming a fit. Scientists are now asserting that evolution as the explanation for the origins of life is a certified, scientific truth. In a July 2002 issue of *U.S. News and World Report* featuring "The New Reality of Evolution" on the cover, journalist Thomas Hayden stated, "By now, scientists say, evolution is no longer 'just a theory.' It's an everyday phenomenon, a fundamental fact of biology as real as hunger and as unavoidable as death."[2]

Dr. Phillip E. Johnson, the University of California law professor whose impeccable logic has tripped up many of the most prominent evolutionists, has pointed out that this assertion is an illegitimate jump to a conclusion much too large to be supported by its small premise. Science has observed that selective breeding and environmental influences can produce adaptive changes within a species. "But evolutionary biologists are not content merely to explain how variation occurs within limits," Johnson says. "They aspire to answer a much broader question: how complex organisms like birds and flowers and human beings came into existence in the first place." But there is nothing in the obvious fact of species adaptation to justify the incredibly broad claim that all species and life itself are the result of a continuing movement toward increasing complexity. Johnson goes on to say, "Neo-Darwinian evolution in this broad sense is a philosophical doctrine so lacking in empirical support that [Harvard Professor] Stephen Jay Gould once pronounced it in a reckless moment to be 'effectively dead.' "[3]

Theories about the origin of matter and life can never come under the umbrella of true science because they cannot be observed or proven scientifically. Science by definition is limited to the study of nature and cannot reach beyond it. Origins demand explanations that nature alone cannot supply; therefore the events that generated matter, life, and reason are beyond the reach of scientific inquiry. We have no way to get data on these first causes and no comprehensible way to explain existence by the laws of nature. The issue of origins is not scientific at all; it is metaphysical.

Scientists overstep the bounds of their discipline and stretch science beyond its capacity when they probe into metaphysical areas such as origins or claim that God does not exist because he does not register on scientific instrumentation. If there is a God, he is supernatural, which means he exists above and outside nature and thus beyond the reach of scientific investigation. Scientists should not expect to locate God inside nature any more than they should expect to find a cook inside his soufflé. For scientists to claim that nothing can exist outside the natural universe because scientific knowledge cannot reach beyond the natural universe displays an excessive and unwarranted confidence in the capabilities of science. It's like saying nothing can exist beyond the horizon because we cannot see beyond the horizon. Or it's like a fish that claims nothing exists but its own pond. It is presumptuous for scientists to claim that science alone is capable of giving us a complete tally of all that exists. Where data is not available, they should suspend judgment and remain open to possibilities. Scientists overstep the bounds of science when they delve into the question of origins, and they overstep the bounds of ethics when they present unproven theories as fact.

In promoting a philosophic belief to the level of fact, evolutionists have bypassed the normal prerequisites of observation and demonstration. They promote their theory in spite of its irrationalities and in the face of the principle of entropy, which says that things are running down, not winding up. Evolution with its irrationalities would look silly were it not for the endorsement of the scientific community. Yet they endorse it because it is so desperately needed to fill a gaping hole in a prevalent philosophy. Evolution would never have been taken seriously but for the naturalists' need to explain origins without God.

Many scientists believe so strongly in the power of science to determine all reality that for anything to exist outside nature is, for them, out of the question. Yet we have the inevitability of the supernatural staring us right in the face. We can conceive of but two possible concepts to account for origins, and both are supernatural. Either something is self-existent, or existence somehow occurred spontaneously from nothing. By purely natural standards, existence itself is impossible because any explanation for it is beyond comprehension. Yet somehow we are here, and things exist. Even though existence defies nature, science, and rational explanation, scientists steeped in naturalism find any admission of the supernatural unacceptable, so they bar the door against God. They choose rather to accept the existence of matter without asking where it came from and turn to evolution to explain how matter became living creatures.

The willingness of scientists to endorse as contrived a solution as evolution poses an ominous danger to the scientific method and thus to progress in science itself. Once scientists abandon the principle of objective truth, science can no longer be considered dependable or predictable. If the principle of entropy can operate side by side with a contradicting principle of ever increasing complexity and perfection, if matter can produce itself from nothing, if energy can generate itself, if life can spontaneously appear from dead matter, then any kind of magic or logical impossibility may indeed be possible. If the universe is that irrational, we have no way to predict what may loom around the corner because the traditional scientific approach can no longer produce predictable and dependable results. Scientific progress as we know it will come to an abrupt halt.

It is refreshing to find a few oases in this desert of overstatement. Some highly respected scientists take issue with colleagues who make such exaggerated claims.

One of the founding and guiding pioneers of NASA, Dr. Robert Jastrow, asserted that creation was a mystery that science could never explore. He endorsed the view expressed by the British astronomer E. A. Milne, who wrote, "We can make no propositions about the state of affairs [in the beginning]; in the divine act of creation God is unobserved and unwitnessed."[4] And concerning the origins of life, Jastrow wrote, "Scientists have no proof that life was not the result of an act of creation, but they are driven by the nature of their profession to seek explanations for the origin of life that lie within the boundaries of natural law."[5]

Even anthropologist Thomas Huxley, who called himself "Darwin's bulldog," realized that science had no power to exclude a divine hand from the origin of the universe: "I find no difficulty in conceiving that, at some former period, this universe was not in existence; and that it made its appearance in six days (or instantaneously, if that is preferred), in consequence of the volition of some pre-existing Being."[6]

The ruling elite of science, education, and media has largely smothered such healthy breaths of open-minded honesty. They have usurped the name of science to close the doors against all possibility of the supernatural.

WHAT ABOUT THE BONES OF PREHISTORIC MAN?

If we deny evolution, how do we deal with the bones of prehistoric humanlike creatures that paleontologists occasionally dig up? Are they really the remains of evolving humans? If so, do they prove evolution?

Evolutionists insist that such prehistoric remains are indeed proof of evolution. But the bones themselves contain no evidence to force or even suggest such a conclusion. If evolution were true, these bones could be examples of it. However, a person must first believe that evolution is true to have any reason to interpret these bones as stages in the process. The bones themselves have no inherent qualities that require evolution to explain them.

These bones become evidence for evolution only because their discoverers choose to interpret them as such. These interpretations are not objective, however, and they fail to consider other viable possibilities. The fact that bones similar to human or ape bones exist does not prove that they belonged to humans or apes. Such bones may be the remains of creatures outside the ancestral line of either. They could point to extinct species of apelike or humanlike creatures with no kinship to humans at all. We have no idea what other types of creatures may have inhabited the earth in its distant past. To claim that the bones of such creatures are stages in the process of evolution is an unwarranted jump to a biased conclusion.

To scientists who take care to keep their minds open on the issue, the bones discovered by paleontologists prove nothing at all about human origins. In his book *Evolution of Living Organisms,* French paleontologist Pierre-Paul Grassé states, "From the almost total absence of fossil evidence . . . it follows that any explanation of the mechanism in the creative evolution of the fundamental structural plans is heavily burdened with hypothesis. This should appear as an epigraph to every book on evolution. The lack of direct evidence leads to the formulation of pure conjecture as to the genesis of the phyla; we do not even have a basis to determine the extent to which these opinions are correct."[7] Dr. Colin Patterson, senior paleontologist at the British Museum of Natural History, when asked to defend his lack of illustrations for transitional fossils in a book he wrote on evolution, answered, "If I knew of any, fossil or living, I would certainly have included them. You suggest that an artist should be used to visualise such transformations, but where would he get the information from? I could not, honestly, provide it, and if I were to leave it to artistic license, would that not mislead the reader?"[8]

Scientists who are firmly entrenched in the evolutionary theory are embarrassed by this lack of fossil evidence for transitional species that would demonstrate evolution conclusively. Richard Dawkins wrote regarding the "Cambrian Explosion": "It is as though they [the fossils] were just planted there, without any evolutionary history. Needless to say this appearance of sudden planting has delighted creationists."[9] Charles Darwin himself was troubled by the absence of fossil evidence for evolution. He said, "As by this theory, innumerable transitional forms must have existed. Why do we not find them embedded in the crust of the earth? Why is not all nature in confusion [of transitional species] instead of being, as we see them, well-defined species?"[10]

This total lack of fossil evidence for evolution (which is as absent today as it was in Darwin's time) caused Oxford zoologist Mark Ridley to conclude, "In any case, no real evolutionist, whether gradualist or punctuationalist, uses the fossil record as evidence in favor of the theory of evolution as opposed to special creation."[11] Yet in spite of such rational cautions, many paleontologists are so doggedly committed to the theory that they continue to make enormous claims from the barest samplings of hard-to-identify bones they find.

Many people today find it hard to keep an open mind about origins. We all have a natural hunger for knowledge, but when truth is unavailable or unpalatable, too often we season our theories with a dash of data and swallow them as fact. Despite claims to the contrary, evolution is not a fact; it is a theory. Data is often interpreted to support the theory by using the assumptions of the theory as the starting point. The result is a tautology—a closed circle of logic without a solid premise: We know that evolution must be true because we have found the bones of evolving humans. We are convinced that these are the bones of evolving humans because we know that evolution must be true.

Unfortunately, the bones paleontologists dig up do not come with identifying labels already attached. As it is, the discoverers name them and give them histories that fit their theories. Dogmatic evolutionists insist that these bones show us stages in the evolution of humans. Dogmatic creationists might as easily insist that they point to some form of human or ape or the remains of an independent, extinct species. Neither has the right to make such claims because both are depending on the mute testimony of the dead, who tell no tales. The truth is, no one knows what these bones are. All claims are guesses.

WHY DO PEOPLE BELIEVE IN EVOLUTION?

You may think we must have grossly overstated the case against evolution. Surely the theory cannot possibly be as unscientific and unreasonable as we have made it out to be. It is too widely believed and too deeply embedded in the foundations of modern thought. An overwhelming percentage of the scientists, educators, writers, and philosophers in a position to influence public opinion and education are evolutionists. Surely these thinkers have studied the theory carefully. Isn't it presumptuous for us laypeople to challenge the opinions of these influential experts?

We must walk a tightrope here. We must admit our limitations and avoid making claims based on knowledge we don't possess. Yet at the same time we must resist being intimidated by experts with an agenda, experts whose claims resist the application of simple reason. And we certainly should not be intimidated when the label of science is misused to legitimize claims that have no scientific basis.

History shows us that prevailing opinion is often at odds with the truth. And each wave of popular opinion tends to become so pervasive that to oppose it invites the scorn of peers and the censure of the politically correct. It is reported that Galileo simultaneously dropped two balls of different weights from the leaning tower of Pisa to demonstrate that gravity exerts the same force on all bodies. Even after witnessing this indisputable proof, Galileo's university colleagues kicked him out. His discoveries ran counter to long-established principles of Aristotelian physics governing the principles of gravity endorsed by the church and the scientific community. Before Copernicus, all universities taught that the universe revolved around the earth. Though Copernicus clearly showed this theory to be false, the church placed his writings in the index of prohibited books for more than two hundred years because they countered the prevailing view that the earth was the center of the universe. To change would mean to rethink long-held doctrines, rewriting textbooks and revamping curricula. Even worse, it would mean that respected educators had committed their lives to believing and teaching an erroneous theory.

Prevailing opinion can be wrong regardless of how widely accepted it is. But however popular an erroneous view may be at the moment, history reveals that no error will survive for long. By supporting evolution and shutting out the voices of rational alternatives, scientists may save face with their peers and keep their reputations intact today. But when the theory collapses in the future, as it almost certainly will, history will lump evolutionists with those who believed in a flat earth, alchemy, and bloodletting. As Malcolm Muggeridge, British philosopher and editor of *Punch,* said, "I myself am convinced that the theory of evolution, especially the extent to which it's been applied, will be one of the great jokes in the history books of the future. Posterity will marvel that so flimsy and dubious an hypothesis could be accepted with the incredible credulity that it has."[12]

Knowledge has multiplied exponentially since Galileo's time, but our basic human nature has not changed. When truth is hard to come by or hard to take, people still find security in their pet theories. They tend to clutch these theories as children clutch their teddy bears, and it generally takes more than mere evidence to pry the theories loose.

When a theory gains momentum with the opinion makers, it seems that no amount of reason can slow it down and no truth can stop it. When a given viewpoint becomes prevalent, differing viewpoints cannot even be considered and are often repelled with outright hostility. Prevailing opinion seems to generate protective antibodies that attack all independent thought that challenges it. For example, the possibility that any race or either sex might excel or be deficient in any given area can hardly be explored, debated, published, or objectively studied in the present social climate. Any finding that suggests a possible difference in tendencies or abilities will be attacked as a threat to the philosophical ideal of total equality. Regardless of how objective or well documented such a study may be, it is unlikely to get a fair hearing today. Our conditioning becomes so complete that fact has no effect. It is painfully difficult for truth to penetrate the preconceptions of the masses—preconceptions so pervasive that most of us are not even aware that we live, move, and have our being in seas upon seas of them.

How did evolution become the prevailing theory of origins in our most influential institutions? Charles Darwin first proposed the theory in his book *The Origin of Species,* published in 1859. It gained respectability when it caught the imagination of influential thinkers such as Thomas Huxley, George Bernard Shaw, and others who found in it an intellectual prop for atheism. Evolution became the thing to believe for those who wanted to be known as daring and independent thinkers.

Since new and daring ideas are newsworthy, the evolutionists with their new theory became the darlings of the media. When evolution became the politically correct thing to believe among the fashionable and educated, much of the general public began to fall in step without examining the basic rationality of the theory. It was enough for them that the right people already believed.

Most of those who balked at the theory were religious conservatives who clung to the old biblical explanation of origins: special creation by a self-existent God. In time, evolution maneuvered religion out of the mainstream of life and relegated it to the area of irrelevant private belief.

Since then, evolutionists have taken control of the terms of the debate. They have shifted attention away from the irrationality and weaknesses of their theory by illegitimately defining the argument as one of science against religion—fact versus faith. Believers have been labeled as close-minded diehards who lack the intelligence to let go of their outdated religious misconceptions. Even today it seems that the media almost always portray the proponents of evolution as fashionable, articulate intellectuals, while those who reject the theory are made to seem ignorant and unsophisticated.

Evolution rolled into the mainstream of public thought on wheels oiled by an intense public confidence in science. Science has accomplished so much in our time that many have come to think it can do almost anything. Some believe that science will eventually eliminate most of humanity's woes—including death—and create a near paradise here on earth. Therefore, when scientists promote a theory that seems to make the traditional God of Christianity unnecessary, many people do not feel a great loss. They don't feel a need for a god as long as they have science to look after them.

THE SACRIFICE OF REASON

Already in this chapter we have made passing reference to one explanation that may be the hidden key to all other explanations for
evolution. Evolution offers something many people want so badly
that they are willing to sacrifice reason to get it. They want a universe
without God hovering over it, and evolution offers such a universe.

It may seem strange that rational scientists would adopt irrational theories as truth just to avoid the idea of a god beyond the
reach of their science. But many scientists in moments of candor
have admitted to doing just that. One of the most quoted examples
is that of Professor D. M. S. Watson of the University of London,
who wrote, "Evolution is accepted not because it can be proved by
logically coherent evidence to be true, but because the only alternative, special creation, is clearly incredible."[13] To put it in simpler
words, Dr. Watson said we have no real evidence for evolution, but
we believe it anyway because, if we did not, we would have to believe that God created the universe, which we will not believe.

Dr. Watson's statement is astounding. It was a bold admission
that he believed in a theory he knew to be scientifically unsupportable
just to avoid belief in God. His stance affirms our assertion that the
question of origins is not scientific but metaphysical. Evolution is
not a fact; it is a theoretical prop to the philosophy that nature is all
that exists. Dr. Watson's belief in evolution was not scientific; it was
philosophical. His philosophy said that creation was unbelievable.
His science would not support that conclusion, so he adopted evolution—not because it agreed with his science, but because it agreed
with his philosophy.

When scientists such as Dr. Watson make pronouncements
concerning metaphysics or the supernatural, they step outside
their field and do not speak as experts. They prostitute the high

pedestal science has given them as a pulpit for their personal philosophy, and we should give their claims no more credence than if they were made by accountants, football stars, artists, bricklayers, or rock singers.

Lest you think that Watson was a lone voice in the scientific community, other prominent scientists since his time have admitted that they hold to evolution despite its weaknesses because it is their only alternative to special creation. Harvard biology professor George Wald echoed Watson's position: "There are only two possibilities as to how life arose. One is spontaneous generation arising to evolution; the other is a supernatural creative act of God. There is no third possibility. Spontaneous generation, that life arose from non-living matter, was scientifically disproved 120 years ago by Louis Pasteur and others. That leaves us with the only possible conclusion that life arose as a supernatural creative act of God. I will not accept that philosophically because I do not want to believe in God. Therefore, I choose to believe in that which I know is scientifically impossible: spontaneous generation arising to evolution."[14]

Prominent geneticist Richard Lewontin, writing in *The New York Review of Books* in 1997, said, "We take the side of science in spite of the patent absurdity of some of its constructs, in spite of its failure to fulfill many of its extravagant promises of health and life, in spite of the tolerance of the scientific community for unsubstantiated just-so stories, because we have a prior commitment, a commitment to materialism. It is not that the methods and institutions of science somehow compel us to accept a material explanation of the phenomenal world, but, on the contrary, that we are forced by our *a priori* adherence to material causes to create an apparatus of investigation and a set of concepts that produce material explanations, no matter how counterintuitive, no matter how mystifying to the uninitiated. Moreover, that materialism is an absolute, for we cannot allow a Divine Foot in the door."[15]

In the face of the lack of evidence for evolution, in spite of natural laws contrary to it, and in spite of the apparent irrationalities and inconsistencies of it, naturalists assert that the theory simply must be true because it is their only alternative to God. To justify this incredible tenacity, they exhibit a blind but dogged faith that someday the missing links and rational proofs will be discovered and evolution will be vindicated. But if present performance is any indication, it will make no difference even if such evidence never turns up. Many will cling forever to their pet theory rather than open their minds to the possibility of the supernatural.

People do not reject God because of facts and logic; they reject him because they choose to do so. They are afraid of God, or they find the idea of his authority over human life repugnant. They know that once they admit his existence, they must admit their responsibility to him, and they want to retain autonomy. They search for an alternative belief with no supernatural strings attached, and they find it in evolution. If we rose from the lower animals, we have no responsibility to a higher power.

ARE ALL SCIENTISTS EVOLUTIONISTS?

Some signs indicate that knee-jerk acceptance of evolution among scientists is diminishing, and that the stone wall erected against examination and criticism of the theory is weakening. Evolution is showing earmarks of vulnerability as thinking scientists awaken to its irrationalities. By no means have all such scientists abandoned evolution or become believers in God. But it is dawning on some that the theory has insurmountable weaknesses. A few of these have dared to break ranks in spite of the immense peer pressure and academic threats that are often applied to those who will not hold firmly to the evolutionary line. The scientific community shows little tolerance for such independent thinking because the theory is too fragile to withstand it.

Dr. Colin Patterson of the British Museum of Natural History was one well-known example of this new objectivity. On November 5, 1981, he gave an informal address to about fifty of his associates at the American Museum of Natural History. He caused a firestorm of angry reaction among his colleagues when he raised this simple question: Was there anything about the theory of evolution that any of them knew for sure to be true?

Another Briton, Sir Fred Hoyle, said in his book *The Intelligent Universe,* "There is not a shred of objective evidence to support the hypothesis that life began in an organic soup here on the Earth."[16] Canadian zoologist Dr. Michael Ruse, one of evolution's primary spokesmen, stunned his audience at a 1993 meeting of the American Association for the Advancement of Science by admitting his realization that Darwinism is based as much on philosophical assumptions as on scientific principles.[17]

If the scientific community continues to produce such honest thinkers who have the courage to proclaim their findings, the world will soon learn that the weaknesses in evolution are insurmountable. The absolute for origins lies elsewhere. We will take a hard look at this truth in the next chapter.

1. Why doesn't the big bang theory explain the origin of matter?
2. What is the flaw in evolution's claim that life, intelligence, and reason sprang from dead matter?
3. Why must evolution be labeled a theory and not fact or science?
4. Do the discoveries of prehistoric humanlike bones prove the theory of evolution? Why or why not?
5. Why is truth often ignored in the face of public opinion?
6. Why do normally rational people hold to evolution so tenaciously despite its irrationality and lack of evidence?
7. Why is the acceptance of evolution among scientists a threat to science itself?

CHAPTER EIGHT

THE RATIONAL
LEAP OF FAITH

The Bible opens with a sort of big bang of its own. In a concise, ten-word sentence, it gives us the one viable alternative to naturalistic evolution as an explanation for origins. It tells us that all that exists was created by the self-existent God: "In the beginning God created the heavens and the earth" (Genesis 1:1). Of course, to unbelievers this biblical explanation of origins is not credible. They see divine creation as a myth devised to explain beginnings in a way that simple minds could grasp. Others regard it as an explanation that was accepted as true until science proved it false, just as the flat earth theory was accepted until we learned better. Those who continue to defend the biblical view are thought to be uneducated, close-minded, blinded by a religious agenda, or unwilling to let go of the comfort they find in God despite overwhelming evidence that their belief has been discredited.

For other unbelievers, resistance to the biblical explanation of origins has nothing to do with whether it is true. They summarily dismiss anything in the Bible because they are turned off by the attitudes and religious activities of many Bible believers they have encountered. They point to some judgmental, hypocritical churchgoers and morally bankrupt preachers and televangelists and say, "If that's Christianity, I don't want anything to do with it." They are unwilling to consider that the Bible may be true in spite of some people who represent its teachings poorly.

Whatever unbelievers may think about the Bible, it does give us the one viable alternative to naturalism. Unbelievers who are serious about their search for certainty should overcome their conditioned aversion to the Bible and give the biblical explanation a hard look.

Following Reason to Its Limits

Some unbelievers have trouble accepting the biblical explanation for creation because the Bible presents it as a mere assertion with no attendant proofs. If the writer of Genesis expected us to believe his account, why didn't he back it up with facts, figures, and formulas to make it credible? Why not a few equations and diagrams? The words "In the beginning" tell us nothing about how time began. Merely to drop in the name of God as if everyone should assume that he exists gives us no reason to believe he does.

On a casual reading, it seems that the biblical explanation of origins is no more rational than the evolutionary one. Both ask us to assume that something has existed always. Evolution assumes it to be matter; the Bible assumes it to be God. Neither assumption is scientifically provable because the concept of self-existence is outside the realm of science. Why is it more rational to assume God to be self-existent than to assume the same of matter? We have no empirical evidence of his existence, and the idea of a supernatural, intelligent being whose existence has no beginning is pretty hard for a modern mind to swallow. Isn't it just as irrational to assume the self-existence of God as to assume the self-existence of matter? When you get right down to it, doesn't the idea of God defy rational explanation just as much as any naturalistic theory of beginnings does?

Yes, both God and naturalistic accounts of origins are beyond the reach of rational explanation. The moment we face such a choice, we realize that human reasoning capacity has a limit beyond which it cannot reach. We are back to that place on the lawn where we first gazed into the nighttime heavens and grappled with the impossible but inevitable endlessness of space and time. Both believers and naturalists must admit that ultimate origins defy comprehension and either alternative proposed to explain them is impossible for the mind to grasp. We are at the impasse beyond which human comprehension cannot go.

Reason cannot explain origins because, according to reason, everything that exists must be caused, which means that something had to exist prior to it. But this means that behind all causes must be an ultimate first cause that is uncaused and self-existent. The mind cannot encompass the idea that anything could exist without a beginning, which is a necessity in both the naturalistic and the theistic alternatives. The rational mind cannot come to terms with the concept of self-existent matter spontaneously generating life, reason, goodness, beauty, and meaning. But neither can it explain the alternative—a self-existent God who by acts of his will brought all nature into being. Yet one of these alternatives must be true because existence cannot be explained apart from self-existence.

But while the mind is incapable of comprehending either of these alternatives, reason demands that one or the other must be true. And reason is up to the task of choosing between them. It is not necessary for reason to *comprehend* a concept in order to affirm it as truth. Edwin Abbot's novel *Flatland* is populated with two-dimensional geometric creatures living in a flat world thinner than a sheet of paper.[1] These creatures could not conceive of the third dimension of height because it was outside their experience and their mode of existence. Yet as one of them discovered, a third dimension did exist, though he could not imagine the configuration of it. Like the flatlanders, we who exist in a world defined by time cannot imagine the existence of a timeless being unconstrained by the limitations of time. In a time-bound world such as ours, where moments continually succeed each other, moving from future to present to past, all things must have beginnings and ends. The concept of uncaused existence is outside our experience and beyond rational comprehension.

What should we do when faced with such alternatives that defy explanation? Should we flip a coin between naturalism and God, or should we just throw up our hands at the whole question and walk away from it into agnosticism? If we have any backbone at all, we will do neither. It is a fatal mistake to think we should believe only what we can fully comprehend. We should not expect to contain the enormity of absolute truth within the walls of the mind, but it takes courage for one raised in the rationalist tradition to recognize that truth cannot be found until we step beyond comprehension into uncharted territory.

To confine belief to the limitations of the mind is like shielding a growing child from danger by shutting her up in a dark room. She will be safe from dogs and wasps and drunk drivers, but her development will be stunted. She will never experience the exhilaration of sunlight and grass and butterflies. Similarly, our beliefs will be "safe" if we keep only those we can lock up within the walls of our own understanding, but we will never experience the exhilaration of plunging into the giant waves of truth and discovering the reality beyond the horizon of the mind's comprehension.

When people insist on complete understanding before they believe, they elevate their minds to the level of a god. They assume their minds have all it takes to be the ultimate measure and judge of all things. They depend on their intelligence and understanding as their own ultimate absolute. But the human mind makes a poor absolute. Not only does it shut down in the face of the great cosmic question of origins, it stumbles every day over ordinary things. When was the last time your mind misfigured your checkbook or misplaced your car keys? How often does it complete the New York Times crossword puzzle or breeze through the IRS income tax forms? Minds like ours don't have what it takes to be our own gods or to comprehend the existence of a real God. In fact, a god we could understand would not be a god worth having.

To find the ultimate, objective truth that gives meaning and certainty to our lives, we must not close ourselves inside the borders of our own minds. We must find the courage to venture out past what we can fully understand. We cannot understand how uncaused existence is possible, but we can rationally accept the necessity of it. Reason cannot comprehend the possibility that raw matter existed always. And when reason examines this concept as a possible springboard for the existence of the universe and life, it must reject it as failing the test of rationality. Self-existent matter accounts for nothing but itself. It gives no account that reason can accept of the forces and mechanisms that could cause chaotic matter to become orderly and spit forth life, reason, goodness, beauty, and meaning. On the other hand, reason cannot comprehend the concept of an intelligent being who has neither beginning nor end. But when reason examines the evidence, it can accept the concept of God as a rational necessity because nothing less will account for the existence of matter, life, and order. Based on this rational necessity, reason can rightly direct the mind to take the step beyond comprehension into belief.

THE STEP OF FAITH

This step beyond comprehension into belief is called faith. Faith is the passport to the kingdom beyond the borders of the mind. We fully understand that the word *faith* grates on the ear of a rationalist like fingernails on a chalkboard, but that's because of a popular misconception about what faith is. We have been conditioned to think of faith as reason's opposite. Faith is often characterized wrongly as a dogged, unthinking commitment to a belief that is unknowable, unsupported by evidence, or even discredited and irrational.

True faith is nothing like that. We should never exercise faith *in spite of* reason and evidence but always *because of* reason and evidence. Valid faith does not leap into the dark; it steps in the direction that reason points. When reason tallies the evidence and maps the course, it hands the keys to faith to start up the engine. Reason directs, faith acts. Faith takes the evidence reason provides and carries it to a practical conclusion. Faith is the beam from the searchlight of reason. It pierces the darkness where reason points and illuminates the conclusion that reason postulates. Faith trusts what reason tells it must be true. When reason reaches the chasm, it points to the bridge that faith must cross. Reason leads to the altar; faith says "I do." As Biola University philosophy professor J. P. Moreland said, faith is "a trust in what we have reason to believe is true."[2] Blind faith undirected by reason is neither credible nor admirable. It is a foolish leap into the dark with no assurance that it will land on the solid ground of truth.

So, the choice between God and naturalism is not a choice between faith and reason. To characterize it as such distorts the terms of the debate because it pits faith against reason when, in fact, they are allies. Faith is essentially inoperable without reason, and reason is sterile and powerless without faith. It is simply inaccurate to claim that naturalists reach their conclusions by reason and believers by faith. As we have shown above, when naturalists and believers search for origins, both will employ reason to evaluate the evidence and analyze probabilities. When reason has formed its conclusions, both will turn to faith to step out into belief and trust. When people choose God, they take a step of faith. When people choose naturalism, they take a step of faith.

Clearly in a rational universe, these two opposing positions cannot both be objectively true. The true one will have the full support of reason and evidence, whereas the other will require a misdirected leap into the dark. The choice between God and naturalism boils down to whether one's faith is informed by reason or whether it is blinded by a skewed philosophy that throws reason off course. Our task is to decide which choice justifies our faith by having the support of true reason.

We must compare the alternatives and determine which aligns best with the reality we experience. Which is the most consistent, and which is flawed by contradictions? Which squares with what appears to our senses and minds to be true? Which explains the existence of such inexplicables as life, reason, thought, morality, meaning, and beauty? The previous chapters have reasoned that nothing less than God can provide a consistent answer to these questions. God must be the absolute behind all reality, or all reality is utterly inexplicable and nothing like what it seems. This is why we assert with confidence that while the concept of a self-existent God is beyond the comprehension of reason, reason itself finds God to be a rational necessity. The concept of God is not in opposition to reason. It is simply above reason. It is not irrational; it is *super*rational.

While the human mind cannot comprehend God, reason applied to available data tells us that something like God must exist. Unbelievers might get by with their claim of some natural prime mover other than God in a dark, dead universe where nothing but cold, inert matter existed. But not in this universe filled with life, law, energy, meaning, delight, love, and beauty. Such things are beyond the capacity of mere nature to provide. The existence of these realities gives us assurance that God exists in much the same way we know that subatomic particles exist. These particles are invisible and beyond the reach of present scientific instrumentation, but we can infer their existence by effects on atoms, effects that only something like subatomic particles could cause. God is invisible, but we can infer his existence by effects in the universe, effects that only something like a god could cause.

When reason tallies up the evidence, it points to an intelligent, self-existent being out there beyond the reach of our comprehension. Though reason cannot fathom such a God, it strongly affirms the necessity of his existence. British scholar and apologist G. K. Chesterton once compared God to the sun: You cannot look at it, but without it you cannot see anything else.

EXPANDING OUR HORIZONS

It seems that many people resist belief in God because it violates a sense of security they derive from feeling they can know their own universe—its laws, its nature, its boundaries. The possibility of something else out there, something they cannot codify or control, makes them uncomfortable and insecure. Nature has fixed, dependable, predictable laws, while rumors of the supernatural are ethereal, ghostly, unpredictable, miraculous, arbitrary, and seem to border on the magical. Nothing about God fits neatly into the modern world's scientific box, so the skeptics exclude him and reject him. They force him into the realm of fantasy to retain the comfort and security of the domain they have stepped off and fenced in.

Unbelievers with such agendas have tightly closed their eyes and willed the supernatural out of existence even though they have no solid ground for denying it. It makes no sense to close your eyes to a possible truth merely because it seems unpalatable. If it really is truth, it must be faced squarely. It makes no sense to claim that what you cannot see is therefore not there just because you don't want it to be. It is dogmatic and arrogant to make the claim the late astronomer Carl Sagan did in the opening of his TV show *Cosmos:* "The Cosmos is all there is, all there has been, and all there will ever be." There is no way unbelievers can know that the universe described by science is all that exists. It is an unfounded claim based solely on opinion or overconfidence in the supremacy of science. In this book we have explored too many things that science cannot explain for us to settle for such close-minded dogmatism.

If the supernatural does exist, we should not expect to understand it clearly when it touches or invades the natural universe. Anthropologist philosopher Loren Eiseley wrote of deliberately touching a pencil to the giant web of an orb spider. As he reflected on the spider's reaction, he realized that her web was her entire world. The spider had neither knowledge of him nor the ability to comprehend that there existed an outside, superior power that could so invade her world.[3] The spider's limited senses made it impossible for her to comprehend him, while he could study her at will. The higher can understand the lower, but not vice versa.

Confined as we are to the web of nature, why should we think it impossible that our universe may be contained within a larger realm that is beyond the capacity of our senses? Why would we expect the supernatural to subject itself to the limited laws of nature? As Plato postulated, the spirit world that seems to our eyes insubstantial and unstable could be a world even more substantial and stable than our own. This universe of ours could be a mere shadowy reflection of a greater reality beyond it. Our failure to comprehend the supernatural gives us no reason at all to deny its existence.

EMBRACING REALITY

Accepting the rationality of God's existence may not overcome all the obstacles to full belief in biblical Christianity. Many issues in the Bible defy understanding. Some can be explained, and some cannot. Must we understand and resolve all these difficulties before we allow full-blown faith to kick in? Of course not. Once we accept God as the ultimate absolute, we can allow the rest to fall into place on that foundation without specific understanding of every detail or issue.

When we become Christians, must we agree with all other Christians on all doctrines of the Bible? Not at all. In fact, it is impossible to do so because there is no common agreement among

Christians on many doctrines. From the beginnings of Christianity, believers have held varying positions on such issues as revelation, miracles, prayer, providence, pain, and worship. But they remain united on the core belief that God is God and Christ is his son. Because we know we are standing solidly on the ultimate absolute, we can put peripheral uncertainties aside without letting them undermine our certainty in the core truth of his existence.

This *modus operandi* is not unique to believers. Evolutionists committed to their basic premise exercise a similar kind of faith in the details they cannot prove. Many have faith that someday a missing link will be found, that the bones cited as human ancestors are what their finders claim they are, that there is an undiscovered principle of improvement that runs counter to the principle of entropy. But the difference between evolutionists and Christians is that the faith of the evolutionist is unfounded. It is based on dogged and desperate commitment to the untenable philosophy of naturalism. Unsupported by reason, it must be propped up by claims, theories, and arguments that run counter to reason and clash with reality. It is a blind, unwarranted faith that defies reason and evidence. Faith in God is the opposite. With God as the ultimate absolute, all the pieces fall into place and fit together in a rational pattern that squares with the reality we experience.

Nothing about the concept of God violates evidence, reason, or any branch of science. Science tells us that no effect can be greater than its cause; creation tells us that a God greater than the universe caused it to be. Science tells us that nature runs down and dissipates; creation tells us that God made everything originally perfect, but it incurred damage and began to degenerate. Science tells us that life comes only from life; creation tells us that life resides eternally in the nature of God, and he imparted it to his creation. The hard fact that forces us into belief is that life is here, and it is not rational to think it could have arisen out of dead matter. The only possible alternative, unthinkable as it seems, is that something alive is uncaused and self-existent. Nothing less than God fits all the requirements. The case for God is that simple. He is the only possible answer to life and existence that fits into place without jarring the order of the universe or insulting the rationality of science. Reason can rationally conclude that God is the ultimate absolute without need of empirical proof. And faith can step out on that certainty.

If you reject God as the absolute and assume naturalism as total reality, you find yourself in a world that insults the rationality of science—a world of contradictions and illusions filled with creatures that seem to have design, laws that seem to have order, morality that seems to have authority, reason that seems to have validity, truth that seems to be true, beauty that seems to have meaning, and existence that seems to have reality. Yet to naturalists all these seemings are illusory; they cannot be sure that any are real. In spite of the appearance of order and meaning, naturalists must force themselves to believe that beneath the surface all is chaotic, senseless, irrational, mechanistic, and purposeless.

In summary, it is at least as reasonable to say that there must be a God to account for life as it is to say that matter is simply self-existent and life arose from dead matter. If all we were doing was guessing without evidence, one claim may be just as plausible as the other. Both alternatives must admit that the laws of nature as we know them cannot account for beginnings. Both alternatives must admit that beginnings are extra-natural and inexplicable. Having admitted that, the next step is to ascertain which claim best fits reality as we know it.

As we have shown in the previous chapters, reason, morality, conscience, the order of the universe, the concept of beauty, and a sense of meaning all point confidently toward the existence of God. They show a consistent imprint on the nature of reality from which God may be credibly postulated. We have shown that reason, morality, meaning, and beauty could not have arisen in a mechanistic universe. As the previous chapter asserted, such a claim is irrational at its base because evolution is inadequate to account for these realities and is based on principles that run counter to scientific law.

Faith in God is not only rational, it is necessary to make sense of all reality.

QUESTIONS FOR THOUGHT AND DISCUSSION

1. What is the relevance of the first sentence in the Bible?
2. What reasons do unbelievers give for rejecting the concept of divine creation?
3. Is creation a more rational explanation for origins than evolution? Why or why not?
4. What are the limitations of reason?
5. What is the nature of true faith?
6. What is the proper relationship between faith and reason?
7. How should believers handle unanswered questions, missing evidences, and gnawing doubts in light of their step of faith toward God?

CHAPTER NINE

HOW CAN I KNOW GOD?

At some point almost all of us feel a sense of alienation—an emptiness in our hearts. Something is missing, and we can't quite identify what it is. We seem adrift without an anchor, longing for an elusive something that will fulfill and satisfy and give us a sense of significance. It seems that every human being comes into the world with three questions etched in his or her subconscious: Who am I? Why am I here? Where am I going? We are restless and adrift until we discover our identity, our purpose, and our destiny.

When we find the right answers to these three questions, we will find certainty as well. As you may expect, those who have taken an unwarranted leap of faith into naturalism will find neither answers to these questions nor certainty. Their response to the three questions must run something like this:

Who am I? I am the product of random forces operating mindlessly on self-existent, meaningless matter. Ultimately, I am neither different from nor more valuable than a rock, a bug, a tree, or anything else that exists.

Why am I here? Since the universe is the result of a cosmic accident, it has no ultimate purpose. And since I also am a result of that mindless event, I have no ultimate purpose.

Where am I going? Destiny implies purposeful direction, and since purpose is an illusion in a mindless, accidental universe, I have no ultimate destiny. And like the universe itself, I am doomed to ultimate oblivion.

Obviously these answers are far from satisfying. It's no wonder that people steeped in naturalism keep searching for better alternatives in any new idea, philosophy, or psychological mind-set that claims to have the solution.

THE SEARCH FOR TRANSCENDENCE

The longing for meaning and transcendence leads searchers to try many paths that lead to dead ends. For example, we are often told that the answer lies inward instead of upward. We feel isolation and emptiness, some say, not because we lack a transcendent God but because we have not found our true selves. This search for self pervades our literature, our psychology, our movies, and even our humor. A scrawled sign taped to the door of an empty office read, "I've gone to find myself. If I should show up before I get back, just tell me to sit down and wait for me to return."

Popular psychology tells us that our upbringing, societal expectations, religious strictures, and personal neuroses conspire to hide the true self beneath layers of distorting masks that we wear to make ourselves acceptable to those about us. These masks confuse us to the point that we don't know what is real about ourselves. We are told that when we strip away the masks and find the authentic self beneath them, our alienation will disappear.

But it doesn't work. Self-assessment and self-realization do not fill the emptiness. While such exercises may have value as a starting point for understanding our needs, simply finding one's true self is not a solution. We are finite; the self has limits. Our hunger for meaning is greater than our ability to satisfy it. Even if we "find ourselves" and settle down to enjoy the discovery, it will not last. Sooner or later we will plumb the depths of the self and discover that it is too shallow to provide lasting enjoyment.

Another widespread approach to fulfillment tells us to look neither upward nor inward but outward. A slogan from an old beer commercial has become a sort of credo for materialistic and hedonistic approaches to fulfillment: "You only go around once in life, so grab for all the gusto you can." Fill the void in your life with toys, entertainment, prestige, pleasure, and achievements.

But it doesn't work. Stuff from the outside cannot satisfy the hunger of the heart on the inside. Among Peggy Lee's many hits was the cheerless "Is That All There Is?" The lyrics picture the sad results of grabbing for the gusto and coming up empty. Lee sings of expecting to find fulfillment in several highly touted experiences, from seeing a circus as a little girl to falling in love as a young woman. But no experience lived up to its promise, leaving her to wonder, "Is that all there is? If that's all there is, then let's keep dancing." It's the answer of despair, the conclusion that the emptiness is permanent and terminal. Nothing will fill it, so to smother our awareness of it we must "keep on dancing." Focus on distractions. Move fast. Stay busy. Party hearty. Do anything, buy anything, try anything to keep from looking into that terrible abyss in the soul.

But it doesn't work. Just as pains and growls force you to attend an empty stomach, the pain of emptiness in the soul will eventually get your attention in spite of anything you can do to ignore it.

THE MISSING PIECE

If we could create our own truth and validate it merely by believing it, we should be able to fill that void in the soul with whatever we truly believe will fill it. But regardless of what we feed it, we cannot sate its voracious appetite. It swallows everything we throw into it yet remains as empty as ever. We cannot create our own personal reality because a true reality already exists. The void in the human heart derives its shape from this true reality. Like the missing piece of a jigsaw puzzle, no substitute will fit. Unless we find the one piece that was designed to go there, the picture remains incomplete.

Seventeenth-century philosopher Blaise Pascal identified this emptiness in the human heart as a "God-shaped vacuum." Pascal realized that mankind's inner hunger can never be satisfied until it turns to God as the missing piece to fill the emptiness. God is the ultimate absolute who brings meaning directly into the life of every man and woman. God in the human life is the keystone to the arch, the one stone that fits at the apex, bringing solidity to the entire structure and holding all other stones firmly in place.

We have demonstrated in this book how reason leads us to the inevitability of God's existence. We have explained that a confident step of true faith puts our trust in the certainty of that truth, bringing us face-to-face with the God who is the ultimate absolute and the true explanation for the origin of matter and life. Now we want to introduce you to this God. We want to tell you who he is, explain something about his character, and describe the kind of relationship he desires with us. It is in a loving, personal relationship with him that we find the answers to the deep questions about our identity, purpose, and destiny. It is in knowing this God intimately that we actually experience the certainty that we can know intellectually.

The Bible shows God to be completely different from the image many people have of an aloof being who exists somewhere out there in the remote distance. He is by nature both personal and relational. Indeed, his very mode of being is relational. God is a living unity of three distinct personalities who exist in an intimate relationship bonded by love. This bond forms a oneness so close that the three members of the Godhead are identified in the singular simply as God. Though he is one, his oneness is a relationship bonded by the very essence of love.

Just as married couples desire children, the three persons of the Godhead desired to expand and share the love that flows within their relationship. Therefore, God created man and woman—creatures bearing his own image, creatures whom he could love and who could love him in return. We are told that he breathed his own Spirit into the first man he created (see Genesis 2:7). He placed his own life at the center of their being, filling their lives with meaning and love. They fulfilled the purpose of their creation by bearing within themselves the life of God, which not only completed them but also gave them immense joy. As God intended, the life of this primeval couple was one of continual ecstasy and lavish delight.

The metaphors the Bible uses to picture the relationship between God and his people give us an idea of just how warm and close he intended it to be. In some passages he portrays himself as a father, in others as a brother, a lover, or a shepherd feeding and protecting his sheep. Many passages portray the relationship of God to his people as a marriage. The core idea within these various pictures is clear: God desires with his human creation a relationship that encompasses all the joy and warmth of our closest human connections.

God intended love to be the dominating characteristic and driving force of all creation. He created men and women to be relational creatures who desire to expand and share the love he lavishes on them. We were designed to live not only in an upward relationship with him but also in outward relationships with others. These connections can be as diverse as the neighbor who borrows a cup of sugar, the friendly competitiveness of a foursome on the golf course, the best friend who lends a sympathetic ear, the deep and delightful bond with children, the intense commitment and intimacy of marriage. We thrive on such relationships because we were created for connection with each other.

This intertwining dance of love with God and others is what gives meaning to human life. As long as the first couple maintained their relationship with God, his love flowed through them and enabled them to remain in perfect relational harmony with each other and the rest of creation. Bearing the life of God within themselves, their life had ultimate meaning, and they were fulfilled. There was no missing piece.

THE BROKEN RELATIONSHIP

Obviously, something has gone wrong. The idyllic picture we have painted of God's love bathing all the world in blissful harmony and relational fulfillment is far from the reality we experience. If God intended us to have perfect relationships, why do they so often go wrong? Why are joy and fulfillment so elusive? Why is it such a struggle to find God? The answer is that God's original intent has been thwarted in a tragic event that Christian theologians refer to as the Fall.

The Fall was a mortal, self-inflicted wound that occurred when the first created man and woman misused the freedom God gave them. As we all know, no one can be forced to love. Both parties must freely choose to love before love can be authentic. Although God made humans for the very purpose of loving him and bearing his essence, he did not force himself on them. The relationship was purely voluntary. The man and woman were free to choose God and all the joy, love, fulfillment, and ecstasy he brought to them. Or they could choose self and go their own way without him on a path infested with all the pain, alienation, sorrow, and death that would result from alienation from God.

Tragically, a day came when the couple listened to the voice of an adversary who deceived them into choosing to go out on their own. God honored their choice. He withdrew himself from their lives and left them alone to find their own way.

Suddenly, their lives were empty. Without God, they were alienated from their purpose and lost their significance. Focused entirely on self, it took humans only a few generations to lose virtually all awareness of God's existence. They had no idea what they had lost or where to look for it—no concept of who they were or what they were meant to do. Estranged from God, they were left with that ravenous void in their souls and a compulsion to fill it with anything they could find to alleviate the craving.

Having lost the stability of their primary, vital relationship with God, all human relationships went out of kilter. Men and women became like spokes in a damaged bicycle wheel, loosely connected at the rim but not attached at the hub. They still had relationships with the other spokes on the rim, but they were unstable because they had lost the overarching connectedness that gave all relationships purpose. Lacking attachment to God, they also lost their point of reference for relationships with each other. Every person became his or her own god, looking to themselves as their own absolutes and fiercely protecting their own self-interests.

Naturally, these separate points of reference didn't mesh well with each other. As these individual selves staked out their own territory and fiercely protected it, they pushed themselves apart. Their focus on self fostered the pride, selfishness, alienation, anger, and hatred that has infected the human family for the rest of its history.

RESTORING THE RELATIONSHIP

You might expect that God would have washed his hands of those who turned their backs on him and directed his affection to a more grateful civilization somewhere on the far side of the galaxy. But amazingly, he did the opposite. Like the mythical Greek sculptor Pygmalion, God had fallen in love with his human creation and could not bear to lose them. Knowing that when they chose self over God they sentenced themselves to death, God set about to perform a daring rescue.

The second member of the Godhead, whom the world knows as Jesus Christ, came to earth, took the form of a man, died on a Roman cross, and was raised to life again. This act disarmed death and restored to lost humankind the right to reestablish a relationship with God. The emergence of the living Christ from his tomb was the guarantee that any person who chose to come back to God would be restored to a life of renewed relationship with him.

"So why isn't it working?" you may ask. If God came to earth to restore his loving relationship with us, why isn't it restored? Why is he still so hard to find? Why do people still stumble around the planet ignorant of God, searching for something to fill the void in their hearts?

The answer lies in our freedom and God's respect for it. He does not invade our space. We have chosen to push God out of our lives, and he will not violate that choice by pushing himself back in. He has left abundant evidence of his existence in nature and dropped telling clues of it from the supernatural realm. But he remains behind the veil, knowing that if he forces his presence on us, we will have no choice but to believe, and the freedom he has given us will be compromised. We must repudiate our choice of self and express our desire for a restored relationship with God before he will move in.

Our choice of self over God also explains the continuing presence of evil in the world. The disobedience of the first couple opened the gates to evil, and in the name of freedom, God had to let their choice stand. But just as humankind chose to bring evil into a world of good, God now offers us the option to bring good back into a world of evil. We can invite God back into our lives and restore the lost relationship, thus finding authentic love and meaning in spite of the ravages of a world infested with evil and death.

Given the Fall and its consequences, we can see why God is now harder to find. But we can also see that it is not God's doing. As the bumper sticker reads, "If you feel far from God, guess who moved." Despite the multitude of evidences of God's existence, we are too caught up in ourselves, too distracted by our desires, too numbed by our worldly preoccupations to see him clearly. Just as animals don't understand the meaning of a pointing finger, we don't understand the many clues in nature that point to God's existence. But that relentless love of his does not leave us solely to our own feeble devices. Even as we search for God, he pursues us, silently nudging events and manipulating circumstances to prod us toward him. Though we often remain blind to him, he is at all times as near as our next breath, ready at our invitation to enter our lives and fill the emptiness in our hearts.

Reason helps us to find God intellectually and gives us a rational foundation for faith, but reason is not where we actually experience God. As Pascal said, "It is the heart that perceives God, and not the reason."[1] The rational mind affirms God's existence, then passes the torch to the heart. The heart is where we experience life's fullness and enjoy all that gives it meaning—beauty, joy, relationships, and love. The human heart can find peace only when the God who loves us dearly returns to it and fills it with his love.

This longing of the heart is so strong that it sometimes precedes reason. A searching agnostic once said to me that while his mind was in a muddle sifting through all the arguments for and against God, he was strongly drawn to the person of Jesus presented in the Bible. He said the possibility that there is someone out there who loves him unconditionally had such a strong appeal to him that he could not let go of the idea. Inherent in truth is a power that can reach beyond the intellect and touch the human heart directly.

THE CERTAINTY OF GOD'S LOVE

It is not surprising that minds steeped in rationalism want to reject the reality of God's relentless, unconditional love. A supernatural creator of the galaxies who took on a human body and was raised from the dead tends to make twenty-first-century sophisticates squirm. To them it appears to be just another of many ancient myths and legends telling of dying gods and human sacrifices to woo or appease alienated deities.

This resemblance of the Christ story to ancient myths is actually a strong indication of its truth. The theme of sacrifices and dying gods persists in mythology because it addresses something that has always been apparent to fallen humanity. People have always sensed the gravity of their alienation to whatever gods they worshiped and dimly realized that only the sacrifice of a god or an extraordinary human could bring about reconciliation. All such myths were prefiguring shadows that recognized the dilemma and anticipated the solution.

At a specific point in time, however, an historical event occurred that fulfilled the pattern of the myths. God actually did come down from heaven and lived on earth as a man. He was executed for the wrongs of the human race, and in three days came to life again and ascended to heaven, disabling the power of death, and ripping apart the veil that separated humankind from God.

Why should the Christian story alone be true out of all the similar myths that precede it? Because it differs from the others as a shout differs from its echo or a tree from its shadow. This tree is firmly rooted in history. The events occurred at a specific time and place and were corroborated as accurate by historians with no stake in the story's veracity. Furthermore, the coming of Christ and many of the events in his life were predicted in writing—even down to such details as the time and place—long before they occurred.[2]

The claim that a supernatural God invaded nature, died, and rose again is astounding, but we have more reasons for believing it than not. We must not make the mistake of waiting for all the pieces to fall into place before we allow belief to kick in. When probing such enormous realities, we are like the blind men feeling the elephant. Our perspective is too limited to encompass the whole truth. We will always wrestle with troubling questions about God, such as the existence of pain, the concept of hell, or apparent conflicts in the Bible.

These questions have excellent and helpful answers available to the person who seeks them. But even when the explanations don't quite satisfy, we must remember that we cannot expect to understand God any more than Eiseley's orb spider could understand him. Often our objections to God assume that he should think just as we do and should have set up the world just as we think it ought to be. When we encounter a world that differs from our own ideal, we make the outlandish presumption that we have the right to banish the creator of such a world to nonexistence. The only rational stance is to allow perplexing peripheral questions to be absorbed by our rational faith in the larger truth: God is; he defines reality; he gave Christ to die for me; he loves me.

Throughout most of history, humankind has had little problem believing in the supernatural. Widespread rejection of it came only with the rationalist overconfidence in empiricism, which demanded a "show me" proof before belief was allowed. When scientists grew bold enough to declare that what they could observe and test was all that could exist, the supernatural was demoted to the level of superstition. The modern age looked back on previous ages with the kind of condescension the enlightened tend to inflict on the ignorant. The attitude was that those poor people back then didn't know any better, but we now stand in a position to pass judgment on their beliefs. This attitude is not unique to our own age. Every age tends to think its own viewpoint is superior to those of the past. Even the postmodernists have great confidence in their own viewpoint that dismisses all other viewpoints as hopelessly skewed.

While we agree that viewpoints do skew objectivity and admit that we all have them, the universe presents to us truths so monolithic that they tower above all viewpoints. Perhaps we can't pull our feet completely out of the mire of modernism's overconfidence in empiricism, but we can see truths looming above us much larger than reason can comprehend. The fog of postmodernism may blur our sight, but no fog can completely obscure the firm outlines of the ultimate absolute.

There it is. The ultimate absolute is also your personal absolute. Incredible as it may seem, the God of the universe loves you personally and desperately, and he wants to win you to himself. He wants a relationship with you, and that relationship will fulfill you completely and bring to your life certainty, meaning, and joy beyond imagining. He is not only the absolute for the universe, he is also the absolute for your life and happiness. He is waiting for you to invite him in.

JOSH'S PERSONAL STORY: HOW I CAME TO BELIEVE

Believe me, I understand how all this may sound to you. I identify with any impulse you may feel to doubt what we have presented in this book or even to reject it out of hand. I spent much of my early life searching in all the wrong places for my identity, purpose, and destiny.

First, I threw myself into religion, going to church morning, afternoon, and evening. But something was still missing. Soon I gave up on religion as an empty and meaningless superstition. I looked for answers in education, but I quickly found that the university professors had just as many unanswered questions as I did. Then I tried prestige, but the glory of being elected to student offices and becoming a big man on campus soon faded, and I was still empty inside.

About that time I came into contact with a group of about eight students and a couple of faculty members who seemed to have it all together. They had an easy confidence and firm convictions but not a trace of arrogance. They obviously cared for each other and for others outside their group. I was drawn to these people and soon made friends with them.

As I sat talking with some of them, I faced a young woman and asked her straight out, "Tell me what changed your lives. Why are you so different from the others on this campus?"

She looked me in the eye and uttered a name that one rarely hears on a university campus except in derision or as an expletive: "Jesus Christ."

I'm afraid my response was less than courteous. Jesus Christ, God, religion—I had grown past all that. Maybe gullible, superstitious, uneducated people easily swayed by their compelling needs could believe such hokum, but not me. Not any more. I would not believe what my intellect rejected. And I told the young woman as much.

To my surprise, my new friends threw down the gauntlet. They challenged me to examine the evidence—to objectively explore the claim that Jesus Christ is the Son of God. At first I thought it was a joke, but when I saw that they were serious, I took them up on their challenge. After all, I was a pre-law student. I knew something about evidence, and I would soon show them that their whole religion was based on a hoax.

You can guess the rest of the story. I looked everywhere for evidence to show that the Bible cannot be trusted. The task proved much harder than I had anticipated, and the search began to consume me. After months of exhaustive research, I had to admit that the Old and New Testament documents were the most reliable writings in all antiquity. At the end of my search, I found myself standing face-to-face with the claims of Christ.

As you can see, it was not the Bible or historical evidence of its accuracy that drew me to God. It was his love shining through the lives of a handful of Christians who accepted me and cared about me. God's love reached out to draw me into a relationship with my Christian friends and through them to Christ himself. The hard, objective evidence convinced my mind that the Jesus who lived two thousand years ago was indeed the one true God. But it was his love that tugged at my heart and drew me toward him.

The result of my search left me with a pivotal question. Since I was convinced that Christ was who he claimed to be, how was I going to respond? He was knocking at the door of my life and saying, "I love you, and I want a relationship with you. Let me come in, and you will discover the very meaning of life itself and find the certainty you have long searched for." And that's exactly what I did.

I discovered that truth is not an abstract idea or a philosophical concept. Truth is a person. Truth resides innately within the character of God, and we experience truth in relationship with God incarnate, Jesus Christ. God himself is the answer to our search for meaning, identity, purpose, fulfillment, destiny, and love. He is the ultimate answer to all our questions, the object of all our longings. And it's as true for you as it is for me.

Your search for certainty may have begun at a different point from mine, and it may have led you on a different course than I have traveled. I needed to prove to myself that the Bible was accurate and reliable. You may need to remove other intellectual obstacles before you can come to belief in the truth. (The books described at the end of this book may help you with that process.)

I hope that what we have shared in this book removes such obstacles and helps you see that there can be only one answer to your search for truth and certainty. That answer is the one true God, who is objectively real and is the ultimate absolute of the universe.

As you continue on your quest, you may find it helpful to pray the prayer I prayed if it truly reflects the desire of your heart and mind: "Lord Jesus, I need you. Open my heart to the truth you would have me find. Thank you for dying on the cross for me. I want to trust you as my Savior and Lord. Make me the type of person you created me to be. In Christ's name, amen."

QUESTIONS FOR THOUGHT AND DISCUSSION

1. What are the big questions that seem to be etched on every human heart?
2. What are some of the wrong places people often look for answers to these questions? Why don't these answers work?
3. What is the missing piece in the human heart?
4. What does it mean to say that God is a relational being?
5. What prompted the Fall? How did the Fall affect our relationships with God and others?
6. Why is God so hard to find even after he provided for a restored relationship with him?
7. How do we know the Christ story is not just another myth?
8. How does the ultimate absolute become our personal absolute?

Chapter One: Does It Matter What I Believe?

1. Rob Rienow, as quoted in Josh Leland, "Searching for a Holy Spirit." *Newsweek* (May 8, 2000): 61.

Chapter Two: Where Shall I Base My Belief?

1. *Merriam-Webster's Collegiate Dictionary,* 10th ed., s.v. "absolute."
2. We understand that certain kinds of knowledge are considered self-evident and need not be traced to an ultimate absolute for validation. Mathematics is one example; the laws of contradiction are another. This is not the kind of knowledge (epistemological) that we are concerned with in this book.
3. *Naturalism* refers to the theory that nature is all that exists, that there is no higher authority beyond nature and no such thing as the supernatural.
4. C. S. Lewis, *The Abolition of Man* (New York: Macmillan, 1947), 91.

Chapter Three: Can I Trust What I Think?

1. G. K. Chesterton, "The Blue Cross" in *The Penguin Complete Father Brown* (New York: Penguin Books, 1981), 23.

Chapter Four: Who Decides What Is Right?

1. Richard Taylor, *Ethics, Faith, and Reason* (Englewood Cliffs, N.J.: Prentice-Hall, 1985), 2–3.
2. Fyodor Dostoyevsky, *The Brothers Karamazov,* trans. Andrew R. McAndrew (New York: Bantam Books, 1970), 95.
3. William Lane Craig, "The Indispensability of Meta-Ethical Foundations for Morality," *Foundations* 5 (1997): 9–12.
4. Taylor, *Ethics, Faith, and Reason,* 7.

Chapter Five: What's the Point of It All?

1. Rick Gore, "The Once and Future Universe," *National Geographic* 163, no. 6 (June 1983): 748.
2. John Updike, "The Future of Faith: Confessions of a Churchgoer," *The New Yorker* (November 29, 1999): 88.
3. William Ernest Henley, "Invictus."
4. Aldous Huxley, "Confessions of a Professed Atheist," *Report: Perspective on the News,* vol. 3 (June 1966): 19.

Chapter Six: Why Do We Love Sunsets and Symphonies?

1. George John Romanes, *Thoughts on Religion* (Chicago: Open Court Publishing Co., 1895), 29.
2. C. S. Lewis, *The Silver Chair* (New York: Macmillan, 1953), 155.

Chapter Seven: Is the Universe a Cosmic Accident?

1. The word *evolution* is sometimes used in a more limited sense to mean the changes and adaptations that occur within a species. We have no quarrel with this limited definition. We can see instances of it in the controlled breeding of cattle and horses, and in the adaptations of species to their environments. Our problem is with evolution as a theory to explain the origins of life and the species. Throughout this chapter, the word *evolution* refers only to the theory in this broader sense.

2. Thomas Hayden, "A Theory Evolves," *U.S. News and World Report* (July 29, 2002): 43.

3. Phillip E. Johnson, *Objections Sustained* (Downers Grove, Ill.: InterVarsity Press, 1998), 20.

4. E. A. Milne, as quoted in Robert Jastrow, *God and the Astronomers* (New York: Norton, 1978), 124.

5. Robert Jastrow, *The Enchanted Loom* (New York: Simon & Schuster, 1981), 19.

6. Thomas Huxley, quoted in Leonard Huxley, *Life and Letters of Thomas Henry Huxley*, vol. 2 (London: Macmillan, 1903), 429.

7. Pierre-Paul Grassé, *Evolution of Living Organisms* (New York: Academic Press, 1977), 31.

8. Colin Patterson, in a letter to Luther Sunderland, April 10, 1979; quoted in Luther D. Sunderland, *Darwin's Enigma: Fossils and Other Problems* (El Cajon, Calif.: Master Books, 1988), 89.

9. Richard Dawkins, *The Blind Watchmaker* (New York: Norton, 1986), 229.

10. Charles Darwin, quoted in H. Enoch, *Evolution or Creation* (London: Evangelical Press, 1968), 139.

11. Mark Ridley, "Who Doubts Evolution," *New Scientist* 90, no. 1259 (June 25, 1981): 831.

12. Malcolm Muggeridge, "Pascal Lectures," given at University of Waterloo, Ontario, Canada, 1978.

13. D. M. S. Watson, "Adaptation," *Nature* (August 10, 1929): 233.

14. George Wald, "Innovation and Biology," *Scientific American* 199 (Sept. 1958): 100.

15. Richard Lewontin, "Billions and billions of demons," *The New York Review of Books* (January 9, 1997): 28.

16. Sir Fred Hoyle, *The Intelligent Universe* (London: Michael Joseph, 1983), 20.

17. Michael Ruse, quoted by Tom Woodward in "Ruse Gives Away the Store," see <http://www.leaderu.com/real/ri9404/ruse.html>.

Chapter Eight: The Rational Leap of Faith

1. Edwin A. Abbott, *Flatland* (New York: Dover Publications, 1952).

2. J. P. Moreland, *Love Your God with All Your Mind* (Colorado Springs, Colo.: NavPress, 1997), 25.

3. Loren Eiseley, "The Hidden Teacher" in *The Unexpected Universe* (New York: Harcourt Brace, 1964), 117.

Chapter Nine: How Can I Know God?

1. Blaise Pascal, *Pensees* (1660), W. F. Trotter, trans., <http://www.ccel.org/p/pascal/pensees/pensees.htm>, (Section IV: The Means of Belief, 278).
2. For more detailed descriptions of the prophecies and evidences surrounding Christ's birth, death, and resurrection, see Josh McDowell, *The New Evidence That Demands a Verdict* (Nashville: Nelson, 1999).

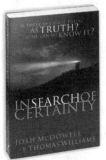

BE CONVINCED OF WHY YOU BELIEVE

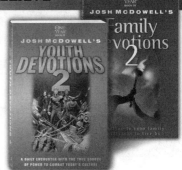

Josh McDowell's Youth Devotions 2
Josh McDowell's Family Devotions 2
to Youth/Families

"We are not fighting against people made of flesh and blood, but against the evil rulers and authorities of the unseen world . . ." (Ephesians 6:12, NLT). More than ever our young people need a spiritual defense. This second installment of Josh's best-selling youth and family devotions offer 365 daily devotional encounters with the true Power Source to strengthen your family spiritually and provide your young people with a resource that will help them combat today's culture. *Josh McDowell's Youth Devotions 2* 0-8423-4096-3
Josh McDowell's Family Devotions 2 0-8423-5625-8

The Deceivers **Book to Youth**

Written in the popular NovelPlus format, this book combines the adventures of Sarah Milford and Ryan Ortiz and their search for meaning, along with Josh's insights found in sections called "The Inside Story."

In dramatic fashion *The Deceivers* explains that unless Christ is who he claims to be—the true Son of God—then his offer to redeem us and provide meaning to life can't be real. This book presents not only the compelling evidence for the deity of Christ but also how God's plan is to transform us into a new creature with an intimate relationship with him. *The Deceivers* 0-8423-7969-X

Children Demand a Verdict **Book to Children**

Children need clear and direct answers to their questions about God, the Bible, sin, death, etc. Directed to children ages 7–11, this question-and-answer book tackles 77 tough issues with clarity and relevance, questions such as: Why did God make people? How do we know Jesus was God? How could God write a book? Is the Bible always right? Are parts of the Bible make-believe? Why did Jesus die? Did Jesus really come back to life? Does God always forgive me? Why do people die? Will I come back to life like Jesus?
Children Demand a Verdict 0-8423-7971-1

BE COMMITTED TO WHAT YOU BELIEVE

JOSH MCDOWELL'S

Video Series for Adult Groups

This 5-part interactive video series features Josh McDowell sharing how your young people have adopted distorted beliefs about God, truth, and reality and what you as adults can do about it. Step by step he explains how to lead your kids to know "why we believe what we believe" and how that is truly relevant to their everyday lives. This series provides the perfect launch for your group to build the true foundation of Christianity in the lives of the family, beginning with adults.

The series includes 5 video sessions of approximately 25 minutes each, a comprehensive Leader's Guide with reproducible handouts, the *Beyond Belief to Convictions* book, and a complimentary copy of *The Deceivers* NovelPlus book. (Also available on DVD.)
Belief Matters Video Series 0-8423-8018-3

Video Series for Youth Groups

Combining a powerful message, compelling video illustrations, and captivating group activities, this series will enable you to lead your students to this convincing conclusion: the ways of the world do not produce true meaning in life—only Christ as the true Son of God can transform our "dead lives" into a dynamic and meaningful life in relationship with him. Josh and Ron have created this interactive series to incite a revolution—a revolution to transform your young people into a generation of sacrificial and passionate followers of Christ. As a foundational building block of Christianity this series offers overwhelming evidence that Christ is the Messiah and challenges each student to commit totally to him.

The series includes 5 dramatic video illustrations, Leader's Guide of teaching lessons with reproducible handouts for group activities, and *The Deceivers* NovelPlus book. (Also available on DVD.) ***The Revolt Video Series*** 0-8423-8016-7

Begin Your **CROSSCULTURE**™ Revolution at www.BeyondBelief.com

BE CHANGED BY WHO YOU BELIEVE

Workbook for Adult Groups

Combining interactive group discussion with daily activities, this workbook helps you overcome the distorted views of Christ and biblical truth held by most children and youth today. It will help you lead them to a fresh encounter with the "God who is passionate about his relationship with you" (Exodus 34:14, NLT). The daily activities reveal a credible, real, and relevant Christ you can share with each family member.

The workbook study provides 8 solid group teaching sessions for the weekly at-home assignments to model the message before others. *Belief Matters Workbook* Wkbk: 0-8423-8010-8 Ld. Gd: 0-8423-8011-6

Workbook for Youth Groups

When your students reject the world's counterfeit way of life, what will life in Christ really be like for them? This 8-session course helps each of your students realize that new life in Christ is about transformation, about belonging to Christ and one another in his Body, about knowing who they really are, and about living out their mission in life.

The Revolt Workbook is an 8-session youth group interactive course followed up with students engaging in two daily exercises per week. This study is the perfect follow-up to the companion *Revolt Video Series*. *The Revolt Workbook* Wkbk: 0-8423-7978-9 Ld. Gd: 0-8423-7979-7

Workbook for Children's Groups

To raise up the next generation of committed followers of Christ, we must start when they are young. These workbooks for children grades 1–3 and grades 4–6 present the foundational truth of why Christ came to earth. Written in simple terms, they lead your children to realize why doing wrong has separated them from God and why only Christ can bring them into a close family relationship with God.

In 8 fun-filled sessions, your children will learn why Christ is the true way and all other ways are false. These sessions lead children to a loving encounter with the "God who is passionate about his relationship with [them]" (Exodus 34:14, NLT).

True or False Workbook Younger Wkbk: 0-8423-8012-4 Older Wkbk: 0-8423-8013-2 Ld. Gd: 0-8423-8014-0

Contact your Christian Supplier to obtain these resources and begin the revolution in your home, church, and community.

JOSH McDOWELL

 never intended to be a defender of the Christian faith. In fact, his goal was just the opposite. As a skeptic at Kellogg College in Michigan, he was challenged by a group of Christian students to intellectually examine the claims of Christianity. He accepted the challenge and set out to prove that Christ's claims to be God and the historical reliability of Scripture could be neither trusted nor accurately verified. The evidence he discovered changed the course of his life. He discovered that the Bible was the most historically reliable document of all antiquity and that Christ's claim that he was God could be objectively verified. When Josh was brought face-to-face with the objective and relevant truth of Christ and his Word, he trusted in Christ as the Son of God and his personal Savior.

Josh transferred to Wheaton College and completed a bachelor's degree in language. He went on to receive a master's degree in theology from Talbot Theological Seminary in California. In 1964 he joined the staff of Campus Crusade for Christ (CCC) and eventually became an international traveling representative for CCC, focusing primarily on issues facing today's young people.

Josh McDowell has spoken to more than seven million young people in eighty-four countries, including more than seven hundred university and college campuses. He has authored or coauthored more than sixty books and workbooks with more than thirty million in print worldwide. Josh's most popular works are *The New Evidence That Demands a Verdict*, *More Than a Carpenter*, *Why True Love Waits*, *Right from Wrong* book and workbook series, as well as *Beyond Belief to Convictions*.

Josh has been married to Dottie for more than thirty years, and they have four children. The McDowells live in Dallas, Texas.

THOMAS WILLIAMS took early training to

be a minister but turned instead to art and writing. His seven books include fiction, theology, and drama, among them the acclaimed novels *The Crown of Eden* and *The Devil's Mouth* in the Seven Kingdoms Chronicles series. Owning his own art studio for twelve years, he designed or illustrated more than 1500 book covers for many of the major Christian publishers. He served as executive art director for Word Publishing for fourteen years and is a five-time winner of the Christian Booksellers Association's best book-jacket award. His painting of C. S. Lewis hangs in the Wade Collection at Wheaton College. He now writes full-time and provides creative consulting services to book publishers.

Tom teaches in his church and has twice served in the leadership of his congregation. He and his wife, Faye, have three married daughters and eight grandchildren. They live in Granbury, Texas, near Fort Worth.